Public Sociology Capstones

Social science departments, both nationally and internationally, market boundless career destinations for their graduates but fail to identify the pathways to these lucrative destinations, and appear oblivious to the social forces that threaten their existence, such as the discerning parent's investment in their offspring's education and mounting individual student debt. This book responds to these social forces, drawing on Michael Burawoy's model of Public Sociology to show how a research-centred experiential internship provides opportunities for students to draw on their prior learning and realise their potential to create pathways towards employment. The author demonstrates how a specific, research-based course leading to employment with a non-government organisation or government department was evaluated and incrementally developed, giving voice to its multiple beneficiaries. Designed for university teachers, this book will appeal to those in social science departments who are using an internship, service learning or capstone model for their senior undergraduate classes.

Martin Tolich is Associate Professor of Sociology at the University of Otago, New Zealand. He is the co-editor of *Qualitative Ethics in Practice* and *Social Science Research in New Zealand* and the co-author of *Planning Ethically Responsible Research* and *Getting Started: An Introduction to Research Methods*.

Public Sociology Capstones
Non-Neoliberal Alternatives to Internships

Martin Tolich

Routledge
Taylor & Francis Group

LONDON AND NEW YORK

First published 2018 by Routledge

2 Park Square, Milton Park, Abingdon, Oxfordshire OX14 4RN

52 Vanderbilt Avenue, New York, NY 10017

Routledge is an imprint of the Taylor & Francis Group, an informa business

First issued in paperback 2020

British Library Cataloguing-in-Publication Data
A catalogue record for this book is available from the British Library

Library of Congress Cataloging-in-Publication Data
A catalog record has been requested for this book

ISBN: 978-0-8153-6032-2 (hbk)
ISBN: 978-0-367-60712-8 (pbk)

Typeset in Times New Roman
by Deanta Global Publishing Services, Chennai, India

To the parents I met at the Humanities graduation at the University of Otago in 2008 who asked me what their children could do with a degree in Sociology. It has taken a decade to formulate but this book is my answer. With thanks.

Contents

1 Mapping undergraduate pathways, not destinations

This book outlines the creation of a Public Sociology Capstone course I have taught at the University of Otago since 2012. Each iteration of the course is described below, and there is yet still room for improvement.

This book has two trigger points. The first occurred in 2007 when the Christchurch Press (Editorial, 2007) mocked Canterbury University's Bachelor of Arts (BA) programme, seeing it as standing for "bugger all" and a weak cop-out for an education. Johnson (2011) reports that the College of Arts administration at the University of Canterbury, lacking financial and popular support, realised the need to demonstrate the real-worth applicability of the BA. The answer they developed was an internship program they labelled *work integrated learning*, designed to both counter the negative commentary and, eventually, to work with and capitalise on the university's neoliberal investment.

The purpose of the Canterbury University work integrated learning innovation was to create a course where students could learn about themselves and the world of work. Johnson saw this as well suited to the current local economic situation (Johnson, 2011, 175), and was both the course controller of the innovation and the researcher who evaluated the course. She reports that her students saw knowledge and its value as a commodity to be acquired, to be hoarded and, ultimately, to be bartered in the marketplace of salaries and prestige.

Johnson (2011, 176) concluded the mingling of education and industry objectives invites questioning around the purpose of a university education. What is the role of a university? Johnson says that if you look at education through an emancipatory lens, education should do more than just train workers. The internship course had the potential to generate citizens who work for their social justice rather than conform to the status quo. The outcomes were not what she had hoped (Johnson, 2011, 179).

All interns articulated a deep investment in neoliberal market-based ideologies, this in spite of the various [social emancipatory] targeted readings ... that framed challenges to neoliberal ideals.

In sum, Canterbury University's social science internships reproduced students with a sense of their own entitlement and privilege rather than political disquiet. This sentiment or outcome is not the promise of social science; Sociology students look outward, trained to help others and to understand the way the social world works and how it might be changed for the better. That is what Johnson wanted to achieve but could not. She drew on others to transcend self-obsession (2011, 177):

> Conceived through these [Freirean/Deweyan] emancipatory lenses, education … has the potential to generate citizens/professionals who work for social justice rather than reproducing conformity to the status quo. In the Freirean/Deweyan conceptualisation, education should emancipate it citizenry to help them to become active moral agents.

The second trigger point occurred in 2008 when I met with a few Sociology students' parents over a cup of coffee before graduation. Parents shared concerns about students graduating with "bugger all," asking me what their son or daughter could do with a BA in Sociology. I had no immediate answer other than to say that their children's course of study did not lead to a specific market vocation such as teaching or accountancy, yet their achievement was certainly not without substance. Neither I nor those parents were impressed with this answer.

This book spans a decade, as I fleshed out an answer. Outlining destinations for these students and parents, however, is not the goal of this book. While employment potential for Sociology graduates is indeed limitless, *destinations are not pathways*.

These parents did not see Sociology as a route to employment. They did not buy the argument that their children were learning about society and that this would lead to employment—they are not alone. Sociology undergraduates ask similar questions: What can they do with Sociology beyond providing an academic critique of sociological research and society? The question is a global phenomenon (Finkelstein, 2009, 90).

Students at Clark University in Massachusetts ask similar questions and are promised destinations: "What can I do with a degree in Sociology?"

> Because of the emphasis placed upon critical thinking, analytic and communicative skills, and methodological training, students majoring in Sociology are well equipped to enter a variety of occupations, as well as professional and graduate schools. Sociology majors have gone to law school, medical school, social work, and business school. Others have become marketing analysts, government policy analysts, university administrators and political consultants.
>
> ("Sociology Department at Clark University," n.d.)

This speculative uncertainty may be the nature of a BA degree (Spalter-Roth et al., 2010). English, Geography and Anthropology BA graduates also experience uncharted pathways towards employment. This situation is not ideal in an economic environment where education is accompanied by significant cost and leaves students and their families in debt (Finkelstein, 2009).

Sociology is not a vocational degree like social work or education. Social work and education students do not ask where their degrees will lead to as their pathways are prescribed for them. These students, subject to demand, will be employed as social workers or teachers. Moreover, academic institutions place undergraduates in vocational settings, immersing them in the real-world situations, which allows them to quickly discover if this vocation is for them and if they are for it. Social work students at the University of Otago spend 60 days on placement in both their third and fourth years of study. Trainee teachers also spend multiple hours in situ. University of Canterbury primary school trainees spend six weeks in the classroom during year one, and ten weeks in the classroom during years two and three ("Teacher education timetables, orientation and course groups," n.d.). Sociology's burden is that it offers its students employment potentials but no vocational pathways to get them there.

Before this Public Sociology Capstone initiative began, Sociology students at the University of Otago spent no time "on placement", and were socialised by the vagaries of the "promise of sociology" (Mills, 2000) or "sociology as a humanistic perspective" (Berger, 1963), or, more recently, "sociology as a martial art" (Bourdieu, 2010). Bourdieu warns undergraduates about the power of the discipline:

> I often say sociology is a martial art, a means of self-defense. Basically, you use it to defend yourself, without having the right to use if for unfair attacks.

Bravado aside, these promises and perspectives do not translate into an employment pathway (Finkelstein, 2009, 93). Sociology offers only destinations. Auckland University's website *Sociology and your career* states:

> Sociology develops analytical and research skills. Sociology graduates have careers in policy analysis, central and local government, the media and journalism, social and health research, business, marketing and union advocacy.

> ("Sociology," n.d.)

Similarly, the Sociology website of the University of California at San Diego is one of many sites which promises its Sociology graduates limitless employment destinations:

One of the virtues of a major in sociology is flexibility in the job market. Actual entry-level job titles of UCSD sociology graduates show this diversity; operations planner for a defense firm, program assistant for a social service agency, teacher, programmer, production coordinator for a publishing firm, social worker for a large, local health agency, communications technician for a telecommunications company, sales representative, analyst, and health intake counselor.

("Career Paths with Sociology," n.d.)

In general, it is assumed that a standard curriculum in Sociology provides students with abilities and skills necessary to be successful in these employment destinations (Finkelstein, 2009, 93).

I too am guilty of suggesting destinations rather than pathways. In 2006, I successfully sought funding from the Sociological Association of Aotearoa New Zealand (SAANZ) to make a three-minute video titled *Sociology: Where can it take you?* As the title suggests, the video reproduces a destination rather than a pathways model. The video depicts successful sociologists in important roles including the Hon. Steve Maharey, then the Minister of Education; Sheryl Hann, researcher for Women's Refuge; and Andrew Butcher, a senior research officer for the non-government organisation *Asia New Zealand*. Parents, high school students and current undergraduates should take heart that the progression from a university degree in Sociology to important employment positions is possible. In retrospect, the video's flaw is too obvious: it does not discuss how Sociology undergraduates' formal education might allow them to make the transition from the university to meaningful employment. Nor does it provide evidence that a degree in Sociology can leap the "gigantic chasm between what they had learned in class and what they actually experienced on the job" (Finkelstein, 2009, 99).

If parents were one prod to establish pathways, not destinations, the right-wing National government was another. In 2012, the New Zealand government announced plans to collect data on employment outcomes, using Inland Revenue Department data to monitor the employability of university graduates. I wondered how Sociology in New Zealand would fare in what was becoming the equivalent of "national standards" or league tables for the social sciences. What is the average income for Sociology graduates? *The Dominion Post* (March 13, 2012) reported the Minister's aspiration to league table graduate incomes by discipline:

[Tertiary Minister Stephen] Joyce said the scheme had been set up to help students make better choices about the courses they studied. It would eventually show the income of graduates five years after they finished a course. Choosing the wrong courses started for some students at secondary schools, he said. Widening the school curriculum in 2010 had been "the right thing" to do because it encouraged a lot more students to stay in school.

(Hartevelt, 2012)

Since that time, humanities funding has not matched the increases in funding for STEM (science, technology, engineering and mathematics) education. High school students and their parents know this and will soon have access to data that stipulates the likely average income for Sociology graduates. In 2012, I wondered if this knowledge would affect parents' investment in their children's tertiary education and the government's investment in the discipline of Sociology. Ironically, the Joyce report may expose Sociology's speculative promise of lucrative employment destinations as smoke and mirrors. Throughout this book, I respond to (and explain) the neoliberal sentiment embedded in Minister Joyce's comments using W. I. Thomas' (1923) classic truism: "if you define something as real, it is real in its consequences." If government policy defines the funding agenda, alternatives find little oxygen. It was within this environment I put forward a Public Sociology Capstone as a non-neoliberal alternative for undergraduate Sociology students' education.

I dedicate this book to those parents I met at graduation in 2008, and I use these ten chapters to describe how I reflected, if not agonised, on their question and came up with a solution that both I and my students find enriching.

Chapter 1, Mapping undergraduate pathways, not destinations deconstructs myths about the BA degree. Sociology departments, both nationally and internationally, market boundless career destinations for their graduates, but fail to identify *the pathways* to these lucrative destinations. The chapter responds to these social forces by presenting the motivations for the establishment of what I originally and mistakenly labelled a research-based internship in a remote New Zealand university, isolated from ideal placements in government ministries or non-government organisation headquarters. The Sociology department at the University of Otago is the southernmost Sociology department in the world.

Chapter 2, Public Sociology Capstones backgrounds the two major concepts used to create this course of study as a hybridisation of Public Sociology (Burawoy, 2004) and capstones (Hauhart & Grahe, 2015). The fundamental feature of a Public Sociology is researching others' problems. The fundamental feature of a capstone course is prior knowledge from previous classes. My students had previously learned skills, and the research project offered by the community liaison allowed them to road test this knowledge by outreaching to the community. They did this outreach in teams of three students.

Chapter 3, The neoliberal intern provides a review of neoliberalism and internships. Neoliberalism has become the dominant discourse of the modern university, as have internships. Perlin's (2012) *Intern Nation* characterises internships as "How to earn nothing and learn little in the brave new economy," and notes that they are rapidly expanding as a form of education. University internships embody neoliberal values; they are engineered to have the student maximise the investment in him or herself. Public Sociology Capstones, on the other hand, focus the student to use and hone his or her skills to find solutions for others' problems.

Chapter 4, Initial responses to the Public Sociology Capstone captures how the students experienced the course first taught in 2012.[1] There was some success, but mostly failure. The positive outcome reported by students was a considerable increase in their confidence, particularly in regard to their abilities typical of professional sociologist researchers. Having said that, the ability of this cohort to describe their activities as sociologist researchers remained variable. The chapter ends by reflecting on how the course could be taught more effectively if I was more hands-off in the writing of the ethics applications for students' projects ahead of time.

Chapter 5, Overreaching community organisations reviewed the five community collaborators' experiences of taking part in the students' projects in 2012. This review led to many changes in the way the class was organised and what part of the course the community collaborators were involved in. Surprisingly, the literature review is seen by the students as a means to an end, but many in the community had little access to the university databases or its extensive library and saw the literature review as an end in itself, maybe more important than the output the students deliver. What the community organisers also wanted was to be more involved in the students' projects. My erroneous assumption was that I did not want to burden them. I was wrong.

Chapter 6, Fostering student responsibility for others outlines the response I made to how the students and the community groups described the course in Chapters 4 and 5. Together, they led to major incremental changes in 2013 and 2014. These changes effectively made me dismantle the ethics application scaffolding which previously had me planning the complete research design for each project prior to the students beginning the semester. Since 2013, the ethics information sheet was written by the students and the application used a low-risk application process, allowing the students to take more responsibility for the projects. In 2014, more scaffolding was dismantled; the most notable change evident in the course was that the students could choose an organisation they wanted to work for. The 2014 students' reflective journals reported how they were assuming more responsibility for their projects. Whereas this responsibility for their project emerged by week 13 in 2013, it was evident by the fourth week in 2014.

Chapter 7, Getting it nearly right: Public Sociology Capstone 2017 was the sixth iteration of the course and had *more and less scaffolding*, capturing my changing role in the students' learning and skill development. First, more scaffolding was needed when teaching the 2017 students as the expectation that the students present their final report publicly exposed some weaknesses in their oral preparation. Additional scaffolding was also evident in the students' first reflective journal, which had them build a learning and skills development portfolio (see Appendix C). The portfolio was similar to an annotated CV. The students listed the 20 courses they had taken at university and gave a brief summary of the learning and skills development in each.

Chapter 8, Messy, creative coaching discusses significant changes made in pedagogy in the 2017 course. There was less scaffolding as I began to conceive of my role more as a coach than a teacher. Subsequently, after the 2017 course, I took a professional development course offered by the university and now fully understand the nuance of how a coach is more a facilitator of another's process rather than a directive of that process. In hindsight, I had unknowingly been coaching for some time. This transition to a coach in charge of a scaffolded class resonates in Harford's (2016) book *Messy: How to be Creative and Resilient in a Tidy-Minded World*. Harford claims that great learning can develop as *a confusing situation always grabs the attention*. By 2017, I realised that messiness was a pedagogy that fit Public Sociology Capstones but not necessarily university student evaluations that ask "how organised was the course?"

Chapter 9, Like sherbet dropped in lemonade:[2] *Students' stories* is a success story. It provides insight into both the range of research techniques employed by the students—observation, surveys and unstructured interviews—and the intensity of the students' experiences that, at times, destabilised them to the point of questioning their legitimacy as social science researchers. The chapter's two entries are combined and drawn together in a duo ethnography written by two students who worked for the organisation Dunedin Rape Crisis in 2014 and 2015. While these students worked on different projects—collating surveys and interviewing referral agencies—when sharing their stories in my office, we discovered that they had the same transformative research experience when presenting their novel results to the organisation. Their duo ethnography was as much about the projects Rape Crisis Dunedin set for them as it was about learning to question both their original research questions and themselves.

Chapter 10, Learning outcomes 2012–2017 reviews how I learned to teach the Public Sociology Capstone from my students, their community liaisons and the students' parents. When combined, this summation explains why the Public Sociology Capstone is a necessary educational pathway for Sociology majors.

The six Appendices provide examples of resources used to teach the course.

Notes

1 All research conducted in this book had ethics approval from the University of Otago Human Ethics Committee. This includes research conducted by the lecturer with his students or the clients. Additionally, all of the students' research had gained ethics approval.
2 Lemonade is 7Up or Sprite in the USA.

2   Public Sociology Capstones

This book is a hybrid of two concepts, Public Sociology (Burawoy, 2004) and capstones (Hauhart & Grahe, 2015). In his presidential address to the American Sociological Association, Michael Burawoy refocused his ethnographic research emphasis away from workplaces in Zambia, Chicago, Poland and Russia inward toward a Sociology of the discipline itself. Burawoy's central claim was that there was a "growing gap between the [professional] sociological ethos and the world we study" (Burawoy, 2005, 7). His new emphasis was a critique of sociological research that he fit into a quadrant.

	Academic Audience	Extra Academic Audience
Instrumental	Professional Sociology	Policy Sociology
Reflexive	Critical Sociology	Public Sociology

Each quarter of the quadrant was important to Sociology, but Burawoy sought to advance Public Sociology, the interaction between sociologists and an audience of public(s). He did not seek to denigrate the other quarters by promoting Public Sociology but instead made what had become invisible visible. Public Sociology exemplars he highlighted were Robert Bellah's et al. (1985) *Habits of the Heart*, David Riesman's (1950) *The Lonely Crowd* and W.E.B Du Bois' (1903) *The Souls of Black Folk*. What these books have in common is that they were written by sociologists but were read beyond the academy and became the vehicle of a public discussion about the nature of US society (Burawoy, 2004, 7). For Burawoy, this was the promise of Public Sociology.

Policy Sociology also interacts with an audience external to the academy but its relationship is different. The norm in Policy Sociology is to contract for payment to write social policy for external audiences.

Of the sociologies in the quadrant, Professional Sociology is the strongest. It is made up of the professional sociological associations worldwide and the hundreds of Sociology departments around the world. Audiences for Professional Sociology and Critical Sociology are traditionally within the academy. A feature of either is peer review and publications in reputable journals. The impact of these scholarly outputs is measured in impact statements, how often a publication is cited by others. In contrast, a review of a Public Sociology output is in the hands of the public. For Public Sociology to have an impact, its findings need to resonate with the community or organisation.

Burawoy claims Sociology's first *public* are its students and he notes an unfortunate tension between Public Sociology and Professional Sociology. He laments that students often attracted to Sociology because of their own activism as public sociologists are tamed by their undergraduate and postgraduate studies within the Professional Sociology quadrant. Their activism is restrained by the requirements to take theory and methods courses and to pass exams. Although Burawoy does not make a connection to his edited volume, written by his Sociology postgraduate students at University of California, Berkeley, the book collection *Ethnography Unbound: Power and Resistance in the Modern Metropolis* has the hallmarks of students performing Public Sociology.

A subtlety of Public Sociology and fundamental to the Public Sociology Capstone pedagogy is this relationship with the audience. Burawoy turns the source of sociological away from itself:

> The challenge of public sociology is to engage multiple publics in multiple ways. These public sociologies should not be left out in the cold, but brought into the framework of our discipline. In this way we make public sociology a visible and legitimate enterprise, and, thereby, invigorate the discipline as a whole.
>
> (Burawoy et al., 2004, 259)

Here he is saying Sociology should not be too focused on itself and what it perceives to be social problems but rather how those at the coal face define or live these social problems. The public are the source of sociological problems.

Burawoy has confidence in his incoming Sociology students at Berkeley who may bring their social activism to their studies. I do not. Many of the undergraduate Sociology students I teach, if left to research what they thought was an important social issue, would navel-gaze at their tattoos or their social media use. The Public Sociology capstone takes these undergraduate sociologists outside themselves and their comfort zones, searching for research projects from local social agencies through a Weberian frame. This works well.

The working definition of emancipatory Sociology I use to transcend self-obsession in the Public Sociology Capstone is Weber's notion of power. Bendix (1962, 290) rewrote Weber's notion of power as "the possibility of imposing one's will upon the behaviour of other persons." Sociologically, these power relations play out in unequal relations between men and women, different ethnic groups and between the rich and poor. The assumption that the powerful command the weak is indisputable, but a sociologist should not underestimate the potent weapons of the weak (Scott, 2008). Many of the organisations co-opted to take part in the Public Sociology Capstone, such as Rape Crisis, Food banks and Habitat for Humanity, among others, maximised the weapons of the weak. Each of these organisations was empowered and emancipatory.

Cook (2011, 7) operationalised "Public Sociology" as a public good, stating, "By taking the knowledge, skills, and techniques of good sociological research, we can improve our communities and help generate a stronger foundation and enhance everyone's quality of life." Public Sociology allows Sociology students to participate in community-based research, allowing them to gain a greater proficiency in undertaking the entire research process (Bach & Weinzimmer, 2011). It would take some years post-2012, as outlined in these chapters, to realise the magnitude of this process.

There was much serendipity in how the Public Sociology Capstone developed. Some serendipity resulted from what I wanted for my students; three innovations or policy decisions were outside my control and on occasion in direct opposition to what I wanted. First, in 2014, I was fortunate when I sought to have the Public Sociology course recognised by the university as a Sociology internship. This was prior to learning about capstones or a pejorative literature on internships. University administrators rejected my request because "internships" was an overly generic term that other competing departments could use. In hindsight, my good fortune was that I was not creating internships in the normal sense. My students were more likely to be domiciled in the library doing their projects. At no time were my students physically located within a social agency or workplace. They met their liaison, usually in the social agency, received instructions for the project and then went to the library to conduct the research. At various times they would visit the agency to report on progress but there was nothing for them to learn from being at the agency.

A second success occurred when creating and sustaining a Public Sociology Capstone resulted from a strategic feature of the University of Otago's Sociology curriculum. Someone else must take credit for this. Since its inception in 2005, a research methods course that I teach in the students' second-year curriculum has been deemed compulsory. The research-focused capstone outlined below is only possible because of this prior knowledge. Undergraduates enrolled in my Public Sociology Capstone do not receive formal research methods instruction in the Public Sociology course, as it is assumed this has already been achieved in prior courses.

Third, when I sought course approval, I wanted the course to be 100% internally assessed. However, because the research tasks were completed in a team, I was required to have a course assessment where 30% of the final grade was a final exam. I was disappointed, but in hindsight, this requirement would prove an advantage. The course was assessed with 50% of the final grade given for the team project and 20% for the four reflective journals. I found that inequalities in either effort or ability among team members were usually offset by what they wrote in the final exam. If I was to design the course again, I would use this assessment weighting of 50% group project, 20% individual reflective journal entries and 30% final exam.

Fourth, capstones are not my creation. In fact, I only learned of the term in 2016 when my university sought to establish internships and capstones as part of a senior project. A google search of the terms "capstone Sociology" in 2017 revealed over 12,000 entries, highlighting their widespread use in the United States. A quick sort of 40 of these produced an array of types of capstones. The core idea was that the capstone represented some final step in an undergraduate's degree. For example, The University of Indiana in Indianapolis described it as:

> In an architectural context, a capstone is the topmost stone that completes a building. In an academic context, a capstone is the final class that completes a student's curriculum. In other words, a capstone is a class in which senior liberal arts majors are required to pull together what they have learned in their previous classes and use this integrating experience to demonstrate that they are capable of doing what they should be able to do as they graduate from the program (think critically, perform research and evaluate others' research, write in acceptable academic style).
>
> (Seybold, n.d.)

The google search revealed a unifying definition of a capstone around the theme that knowledge acquired in previous courses was used to research a particular topic as the culmination of an undergraduate degree. There were variations on the capstone—many were individual projects leading to a senior project or single thesis. Most required some type of reflection along with the output. Boston College's Capstone sought to have students reflect on their education and any disconnect between their undergraduate Sociology training and their future lives (Morello, n.d.). North-Eastern University Capstone did the same, using the senior project to develop the students' sense of themselves as sociologists (Holton, n.d.).

A number of universities offered their senior undergraduates a clutch of options. Humboldt State Sociology offered students an internship, a senior thesis or a community action research project. The latter had three of the trappings of Public Sociology, (1) prior learning, (2) teamwork and (3) working for the community, that **I emphasise in bold**:

> Students who complete a **Community Action Research** project are expected to contribute to **a team-based** research project **studying a community issue**. Topics for projects will change each year, based on the expertise of the instructor. This course will build on the skills acquired in both SOC 382: Introduction to Social Research and SOC 372: Proseminar by conducting real research with community partners. This course is ideal for building applied sociological skills.
>
> ("BA Capstone Planning," n.d.)

The University of Illinois in Chicago Department of Sociology also offered a Public Sociology like capstone:

> **Capstone** course, which provides senior sociology majors the opportunity to engage in a practical, **team-b**ased service project that advances **the mission of a community organization**. Capstone students **apply the sociological skills** they have gained in the major to advance **a project arranged by a community partner**.
>
> ("UIC SOC 490 Capstone," n.d.)

The only university that offered a course labelled a Public Sociology Capstone was the University of the Rockies. This course was offered at the Masters level:

> This capstone course **addresses the application of sociological theory and research methods to social problems or policy concerns in organizations or communities.** Students can either choose from a selection of case studies provided or identify a local organization with an applied or medical social problem or policy issue and develop a proposed solution that applies their learning through an integrative project plan that combines theory, research, and practice. Prerequisite: completion of all required coursework.
>
> ("Master of Arts in Public Sociology Courses," n.d.)

The courses described above were found after I had taught this course for six years and after I had been introduced to Hauhart and Grahe's (2015, 192–193) prescription for a successful capstone course. They summarise the capstone by stating:

> Although we offer a set of recommendations we believe we can help create the ideal capstone course, we express humility in the face of this task ... In our view, the research literature suggests the ideal discipline-specific capstone course is *a research-based course one semester long, **scaffolded** in sequence by one or more required undergraduate research courses, and offered in either a classroom-based seminar format or an internship/practicum format.*
>
> (my emphasis)

Scaffolding is a fundamental feature of a capstone course and is featured prominently in this book. In 2012, the first iteration of the Public Sociology Capstone was heavily scaffolded to the point where it would have been difficult for a student to grasp their responsibilities in the course prescription. In subsequent iterations, the scaffolded structure of the course was gradually dismantled, allowing students to take more and more responsibility for their own learning. What follows are Hauhart and Grahe's (2015, 193–198) ten specific recommendations for a capstone. In the body of the book, I explain how these recommendations matched my Public Sociology Capstone.

1 Create prerequisites for the capstone so that students can work independently without stumbling.
2 Be aware of staff–student ratios by limiting class size.
3 Create enthusiasm by allowing students to select their own topics.
4 Ensure that any large task is clearly sequenced with predetermined timelines.
5 Organise regular instructor–student meetings and wider class discussions.
6 Encourage peer review during class meeting discussions.
7 Make students aware of on-campus resources such as reference librarians.
8 Invite students to make a public presentation of their research project.
9 Encourage ongoing learning by inviting past students to share their capstone journey.
10 Evaluate the course at the end plus regularly, with reflective journals.

It is worth repeating that the contrast above between the ideal type of capstone and the course that I have taught for the past six years is minuscule.

It suggests that I have always taught a capstone course in form but not in name. As if an endorsement, Hauhart and Grahe (2015, 198) emphasise

> that a senior capstone course developed and implemented along the lines [they] have recommended will produce successful student outcomes for the overwhelming majority of students ... In our view, creating a sound design within the parameters we have suggested is the best practice for teaching synchronous capstone course that one can find.

This book documents how the initial course taught in 2012 has been modified by removing more and more of the scaffolding that I initially thought was essential for this course, leaving behind a course where students can use their prior knowledge and take responsibility for independent research. At all times, the student's focus is on helping his or her organisation achieve its goals rather than seeing the course as an investment in him or herself. No attempt is made to elaborate the Hauhart and Grahe model other than to link it with Public Sociology. My contention is that the Public Sociology course that I began teaching in 2012 had all the hallmarks of a capstone. It was never an internship, although I did mistakenly use the term internship in a number of articles I wrote.

The Public Sociology Capstone as it is now called is a three-part process: (1) It allows students who have previously passed a research methods course to test their book learning in the field by conducting a mixed methods research project in a (2) team setting on (3) behalf of a community organisation. This experiential learning model assumes that "students who are involved in educationally productive activities in college are developing habits of the mind and heart that enlarge their capacity for continuous learning and personal development" (Kuh et al., 2008, 25). This three-part process fulfils one of Hauhart and Grahe's (2015) recommendations: *Create prerequisites for the capstone so that students can work independently without stumbling.*

This Public Sociology Capstone is unique in New Zealand Sociology and rare internationally but pedagogically sound. In his seminal *Teaching Sociology* article, Finklestein (2009, 90) argues that "the field of applied Sociology and teaching and learning sociological practice has struggled to develop in the discipline." This idea is not new. A quarter-century ago, Davis (1993) claimed that such an experiential course has great potential to draw together theoretical work from disparate areas of Sociology to serve as a bridge to postgraduate study and help students assume more active lives as citizens and consumers of knowledge.

The Public Sociology Capstone serves as a bridge for students completing their degrees by providing them with specific experience to prepare them for entry-level policy analyst positions in Government ministries or NGOs. For students continuing on to postgraduate studies, the course serves as a short, sharp introduction into the messy and non-linear world of social research. It gives undergraduates the opportunity to put theory into practice by work-shopping their book learning.

At the completion of their degrees, Sociology graduates from the University of Otago are expected to demonstrate a range of skills and attributes including problem solving, critical thinking, self-motivation, being a team member, competence in social research skills, time management and the ability to extrapolate from knowledge and principles to solve new problems. This skill set is remarkably similar to attributes listed in advertisements for New Zealand government policy analyst positions. The following Ministry of Internal Affairs advertisement lists problem solving and time management as key attributes a policy analyst should hold:

Do you enjoy working in a fast past environment with good team dynamics and great development opportunities?

Do you want to:

- hone your writing skills producing a variety of products for Ministers?
- work in a fast paced supportive team?
- develop your policy skills working across a broad range of policy issues?
- prepare briefings and speeches for Ministers on a wide range of issues;
- provide advice to Ministers and government agencies on topics and issues that matter for New Zealand's 200 odd ethnic communities
- liaise with Ministers' offices and other teams across the branch and Department; and
- keep informed about relevant and emerging issues.

In each of these past six years that I have taught the course, I have mirrored the students' activity and reflected on my teaching experience, producing a journal article each year (Tolich, 2012a; Tolich, 2012b; Tolich, Paris & Shephard, 2014; Tolich, Shepard, Carson & Hunt, 2013; Tolich, 2015; Tolich, Scarth & Shephard, 2015), all of which document the success and the many setbacks in teaching the course as Public Sociology. There are lessons to be learned for teachers in those mistakes, some character building, yet each year the course adjusted to these lessons. This evaluation fulfils Hauhart and Grahe's tenth recommendation of a successful capstone: *Evaluate the course at the end, plus regularly with reflective journals.*

The book chapters that follow sequence my learning and document the skills developed to teach this course in the same way the students learned from their mistakes. Teaching this Public Sociology Capstone as a reflective exercise for teacher and students involves a novel pedagogy: each party self-evaluating their learning and skills before, during and after the research experience.

3 The neoliberal intern

External threats to the humanities at Canterbury University were met with the establishment of a neoliberal internship programme for BA students. My own response to the parents I met a graduation in 2008 was to create the Public Sociology Capstone.

The differences between an internship and a Public Sociology Capstone are not just semantic; they are philosophically different and, as captured in the subtitle of this book, non-neoliberal alternatives to internships. Capstones are neither neoliberal nor an internship. Universities market internships as "work integration" or as the student being "work-ready." Neoliberalism tends to focus the students inward, on themselves as consumers and the investment they have made in their education. Public Sociology, on the other hand, by its very nature focuses on the other, namely other people's problems.

Neoliberalism 101

Neoliberalism was ushered in by a New Zealand Labour government in 1984 (Kelsey, 1995). The Labour government was hell bent on privatising the public sector; the shorthand label for it was Rogermomics, a play on either Reaganomics or Thatcherism that preceded and produced the neoliberal hegemony. It was a hegemony based on TINA, *there is no alternative*, a slogan that legitimised the privatisation of the public sector. The fourth Labour government sold the railways, Air New Zealand and any state-owned asset while bringing market forces to bear on the public sector. It was presented as that there was no other alternative but to sell state-owned assets.

Public education did not escape TINA. Changes to primary and secondary school education were outlined in the Picot report (McKenzie, 1999). Rather than having primary schools centrally administered by a government ministry, oversight was given over to school boards voted on by parents. Parents now had choice, a neoliberal buzzword.

New Zealand universities, too, were subject to market forces often captured in the term *user pays*. If students wanted to go to university, they would need to fund part of their education as an investment in themselves. University education was commodified. This innovation post-1984 was new; commodified education had not been my experience when I attended Auckland University from 1978 to 1983, nor had it been the experience of the parents I spoke to in 2008. In Sociology, we call this shift a form of the sociological imagination, where personal biography meets history. This concept captures a shared biography (the parents and mine) and a shared pre-1984 historical moment that preceded the shift to neoliberalism.

I vividly remember enrolling for postgraduate study at Auckland University in 1981. My university fees for the entire year, enrolled in a Master of Arts in Sociology, were $26. The moment was made special by the person standing in line behind me. She was a former teacher of mine when I took politics as a minor in my undergraduate BA. In time, she would go on to be the greatest prime minister of New Zealand and later the Secretary of the United Nations Development Programme from 2009 to 2017. But at that time, Helen Clark was enrolling in a PhD for a minuscule amount of money. Were she to apply for a PhD in 2017, the fees are $6458 per year. Times have changed and so has the social policy that forces New Zealanders to think about the social and economic value of education in terms of an investment.

This privatisation of formally public institutions, like universities, is grounded in the assumption that the private sector responds more effectively and fairly through competition and incentives. The ethos here is freedom and choice, bolstered by TINA. The purpose of education in the New Zealand knowledge economy is to represent a path to individual economic security.

The assumption here is inherent in government policy since 1984; students go to university to maximise their financial return. If so, the students should choose subjects that maximise their returns. In terms of a sociological imagination, the student's biography is not determined by them or their parents but by a neoliberal economic policy that is regularly touted in media sources. For example:

> Yesterday [March 30, 2016] the Ministry of Education released factsheets on the national employment outcomes for young domestic graduates, tracking their earnings and employability for the first nine years following graduation. The information comes from a dataset administered by Statistics New Zealand using the earnings for each discipline based on tax returns. "This underlines the importance of encouraging more students to study science, technology, engineering and maths (STEM) subjects at school and in tertiary education,"

[Minister of Tertiary Education] Joyce says. Joyce says this information will help students and their families to make smart decisions about what to study, "which will set them up for a prosperous future."

("Income premiums for study options revealed," n.d.)

Let's unpack the sentiments embedded in this press release. It is characteristically neoliberal. Students are faced with TINA—there is no alternative but to enrol in income-generating subjects. There is no alternative because the assumption is that students who seek higher education do so to maximise personal incomes. The firm belief extolled in neoliberalism is that all people are created equal and they are free to live their lives without a great deal of interference from the government. Keywords here are choice and freedom, as if each person had access to similar life chances.

If government policy favours one set of learning over another, for example, STEM (science, technology, engineering and mathematics) over humanities, this will undermine the worth of humanities. Fewer students will take the courses and the humanities will get less bums-on-seats funding. This reveals two key sociological concepts. As mentioned above (Thomas, 1923), "if you define something as real, it is real in its consequences." If a budget defines what types of education the government will be funding, the outcome is real. Sociologically, this is not rocket science, it is *a self-fulfilling prophecy*. Within this shift in funding, tertiary education is forced to explore other avenues such as internships to ensure its survival. Making students "work-ready" is a choice presented as if there was no alternative. For Perlin (2012, xi), "The internship has become a new and distinctive form, located at the nexus of transformations in higher education in the workplace."

Internships come to blur the line between the private and the public. They decentralise students, taking them out of the classroom, outside of the university; yet, for the duration of the internship, the university coffers benefit from student fees they themselves do not teach (Perlin, 2012, 8). In other words, understanding internships is best achieved by seeing them as expressions of neoliberalism. The public university education system imbues the students with skills that are then evaluated by a private sector that offers them no guarantee that there will be value added.

Internships 101

Ross Perlin (2012), in his book *Intern Nation*, acknowledges competing tensions in the modern university with the neoliberal investment model undermining traditional education. On one side, he hears mixed messages of who his education should benefit:

From lecterns I heard: Do something meaningful with your life. Give back to those who are less fortunate. From relatives, family friends and assorted advice giving adults, I heard, Get paid to do something you enjoy. From those a few years older than me, It's a tight job market out there. Be flexible control your own destiny.

(Perlin, 2012, ix)

These latter messages he internalised; without an internship featured on his resume, he assumed it was looking increasingly impractical that his broad university education was sufficient in itself to translate into paid employment. *There was no alternative.*

Perlin's internship is subject to historical forces. Andrew Ross (2009), a US labour theorist, goes as far as suggesting that internships are the fastest-growing job category. They are increasingly the first step into a career, as if undertaking an internship is tantamount to a mandatory requirement for entry into the market (Swan, 2015, 31). Perlin (2012, xiv) reports that of the 9.5 million students attending four-year colleges in the United States, as many as 75% undertake at least one internship before graduating. Internships in these numbers are changing the nature of work and education. In the UK, students' employability is of increasing importance as a key agenda item for higher education institutions (Ball, Pollard & Stanley, 2010). In 2010, one in five UK employers intended on hiring summer interns (Swan, 2015), creating a convenient employability strategy that outsources teaching to private companies.

In essence, internships are overwhelmingly positioned or marketed (Perlin, 2012) in terms of an opportunity for learning, but at the same time this learning is commodified and exchanged trading of a student's labour, often for a cashless experience. Universities' promotion of these uncertain exchanges assumes students gain experience in their ideal professional occupation or test organisations (Swan, 2015, 33). The experience assumes, but does not guarantee, that some learning will take place in exchange for work performed (Perlin, 2011).

Like many other academics, Perlin (2012) is disparaging about internships. His *Intern Nation's* subtitle is "How to earn nothing and learn little in the brave new economy." The book is based on his research on interns and his experience as one while in graduate school at the University of London. He claims internships offer

the unrivalled gateway to white-collar work, now backed by government policies across the globe, employers hiring practices, a nearly unanimous academy, and a million auxiliary efforts. How did we get there?

(Perlin, 2012, xi)

Perlin's book reviews interns in the fashion and motion picture industry and in politics, but he begins his critique detailing the Magic Kingdom internships. Disney hires between 7000 and 8000 college student interns per year to work on unspecified menial tasks for minimum wage. Over the past 30 years, the Disney World College program has employed more than 50,000 interns. Perlin (2012, 2) adds context to these jobs:

> The interns work entirely at the company's will, subject to a raft of Draconian policies, without sick days or time off, without grievances procedures, without guarantees of working compensation or protection against harassment or unfair treatment. Twelve hour shifts are typical, many of them beginning at 6 a.m. or stretching past midnight. Interns' sign up without knowing what jobs they will do or the salaries they'll be paid (though it typically hovers right near minimum wage).

This criticism is also found in Kevin Yee's (2008; cited in Perlin, 2012, 17–18) critical memoir of his 15 years working as a Disney employee. Perlin reports:

> These kids are lured to the promise of working Pirates of the Caribbean but ultimately cleaning toilets, or serving hamburgers, although a few do end up working the attractions. They are often lured with the idea of an internship or management, and in reality, they do grunt work.

Perlin (2012, 3) concedes it is not the content of the internships that matters but the context—how the tasks get represented on the intern's CV.

> Should the magic fail, the program at least seems to promise professional development and the prestige of the Disney name, said to stand out on a resume regardless of the actual work performed. Yet training and education are clearly after thoughts; the kids are bought in to work.

Swan (2015, 32), writing from UK perspective, adds another form of disparagement:

> Students, interns, journalists and trade unions agree that internships are exploitative on many counts: lack of pay or poor pay, unstable and insecure work, few tangible benefits and poor quality of work experience offered …. An internship has become a transaction in which experience and learning, and not money as in the past, are exchanged for work performed.

One of the downsides of internships are their lack of accountability. Disney interns get to note on their CV that they interned at the ninth most identifiable brand in the world. Whether they parked cars or flipped burgers does not seem to matter. They had the Disney experience. Perlin does not believe this is enough of a return.

The other downside to internships are its class implications. Work placements are not just about learning about the world of work, but they are a filtering site (Allen et al., 2013) in which students are evaluated through classifying practices that privilege middle-class ways of being. Students are classified as being or failing to be the right subjects demanded by any of the corporations. Johnson (2011, 178) also found filtering.:

> Choice is not a value neutral concept. Indeed choice and the making of choices reveal and situate social location in terms of race, gender, and class, disability age etc. For example the multitude of choices available to and made by a white upper-class woman will be different from choices available to and made by a lower class black man.

Swan (2015) is no supporter of internships, also claiming they structure inequalities. Internships, she claims, are premised on who can afford to take the deferred gratification of an unpaid internship with the vague promise of converting this into a marketable commodity. But at what cost? Interns are widely viewed as being exploited, undertaking menial work, and in return are expected to display enthusiasm and gratitude and put up with a frequent lack of on-the-job training. Another downside of internships is that they offer few tangible benefits, and the poor quality of work experience offered (Lawton & Potter, 2010).

Perlin's (2012) book is replete with examples where interns are promised training and skill development but this is not delivered upon. There is little direct training and mentoring. To succeed in an internship is to strategise the self as an entrepreneur, the ideal citizen (Apple, 2006, 196) possessing the discourse of flexibility, self-sufficiency and individualism.

Neoliberalism values education for rendering people suitable for the market. Internships do this. Students themselves see university education as offering a smooth transition into professional practice (Swan, 2015, 36). University lecturers such as Jessica Johnson at Canterbury University see the role of education differently. So do I. The students in a Public Sociology Capstone may be working for a social agency but their feet are firmly within the university; they are managed and monitored in a highly scaffolded setting, ensuring fair learning outcomes. The students' focus is more on learning that enhances social emancipation for others and their organisations. At no time did my students describe their education or themselves as a commodity.

4 Initial responses to the Public Sociology Capstone

This chapter[1] begins by outlining the structure of the Public Sociology course that was first taught in 2012. From there, students describe how they experienced the Public Sociology learning objectives, assessing what confidence they had in describing the course. The chapter ends by criticising my use of a "high risk" ethics application process that meant students were unnecessarily excluded from opportunities for assuming responsibility for their projects.

In 2012, five local organisations were approached and asked if they would take part in the course. Access to these research sites around the city was based on their proximity and a hunch that they would present an array of sociological problems of interest for the students. They all agreed. These organisations were:

1 The Dunedin City Libraries' Mobile Library (the Book Bus)
2 The *Otago Daily Times*' Dawn Patrol (newspaper deliverers)
3 Dunedin's four food banks
4 The University of Otago Marine Science Outreach for gifted and talented students
5 The University of Otago's Science Wananga (educational outreach to remote indigenous communities)

The Dunedin Central Libraries' Book Bus seemed a vulnerable social service in times of economic austerity, which is worsened by Dunedin's self-imposed 30-year mortgage to pay for a new rugby stadium. The students' study collected voices of the Book Bus consumers and recorded them to produce a short documentary for the library.

The Otago Daily Times' Dawn Patrol Project studied those who delivered the morning ODT newspaper, allowing this invisible group, mostly high-school workers, to tell their story about what they do, how they do it and for what purpose. The project's output had the potential to result in a story about the Dawn Patrol being submitted for publication in the magazine pages of the Saturday ODT, although its publication would of course not be guaranteed. The general line of questioning focused on: What motivates these workers to get out of bed in snow and rain to deliver the paper? Others questions asked: How do they manage or customise their route? What life skills do they develop in delivering the paper? How do they manage dogs and other hazards? What is one thing that could improve the job?

The Food Bank Project investigated the food distribution policies used in each of the four Dunedin food banks. The four students assigned to this site would be expected to volunteer some of their time in the food banks and to interview key informants. The assigned output would be a laminated poster for each food bank, contrasting each food bank's distribution policy.

The Science Wananga Project's population was postgraduate students who have acted as mentors in the University of Otago's Science Wananga. The Wananga is a teaching outreach designed for rural Maori high schools. The aim of the students' projects was to understand how mentors experienced their teaching, and whether it enhanced or detracted from their education and career aspirations. The general line of questioning focused on having the postgraduate students reflecting back on the expectations they had going to the Wananga, and whether or not these expectations were met.

The Gifted and Talented Project studied high school students aged 15 who took part in the 2010 Gifted and Talented programme held at the University of Otago's Portobello Aquarium. They were asked about their experience and what impact it had on their subsequent learning and social networks. Additionally, they were asked what the term "gifted and talented" meant to them, and what it was like being among students with similar abilities as them and returning to the regular classroom afterwards.

The inaugural course in 2012 was scaffolded by incremental stages leading to the production of a single research output for the students' community liaison, be it a written report or something specialised like a pamphlet or a video. This format has remained the same over six years. The four stages were:

- writing a literature review;
- constructing a research instrument (survey or an interview guide);
- coding data in a preliminary thematic report;
- constructing the final report.

These four stages fulfil Hauhart and Grahe's (2015) recommendation to ensure that any large task is clearly sequenced with predetermined timelines. A second Hauhart and Grahe recommendation to make students aware of on-campus resources such as reference librarians was not necessary. A feature of the year two prerequisite course is a lecture from the specialist social science librarian who addresses tips on pre-searching a topic as well as generating a literature review. In the Public Sociology course, students are expected to have mastered these basics, yet they are encouraged to make an appointment with the specialist social science librarian to discuss their new topic. This expectation is based on the students taking the lead to resolve their own problems.

If I have learned one lesson from this course, it is to beware of linear processes such as the four stages listed above. A more realistic step process is to cite Lao Tzu's belief that great things start from humble beginnings ("Lao Tzu Quotes," n.d.). The journey of a thousand miles begins with one step. In year one, I had not grasped that the four stages comprised a thousand micro-steps. In hindsight, I now label many of these invisible micro steps as professional development.

The students meeting the community liaison for the first time to learn the nature of the research project, for example, was a daunting micro-step, as was the final meeting with the community liaison when the students presented the outcome of the project. Neither moment was assessed for a grade or thought of as being one of the four stages of the course, yet these moments were essential to the experiential learning. Students' ability to work in teams was also a major step and not assessed specifically, but it too developed as a novel feature for most students. For many, their ability to work with others to schedule meetings between themselves or with members of their community group was character building.

Each of the five research projects in 2012 involved the students meeting their particular community group to plan and discuss research objectives and questions, interviewing participants at intervals, analysing data and producing reports or resources for the community groups.

Formally, the course had seven learning objectives:

1   To work cooperatively and effectively within a small research team.
2   To use methodological skills and theoretical insights to define an iterative research topic that should be negotiated with the community liaison.
3   To design a mixed methods research instrument that meets the needs of the research question.
4   To present the findings as a written report or other resource for the community group.
5   To gain experience working within a community agency and conducting oneself as a professional researcher.
6   To conduct the research in adherence with key ethical principles.
7   To experience the highs and frustrations of conducting a research project.

The seventh objective is experiential, focusing on the highs and lows of being a researcher. I had presumed that the students' research process would not be linear, but not necessarily iterative either. The expectation was that the process would include many false starts as the students waited to meet with their community liaisons, schedule team meetings and recruit research participants. The military term "hurry up and wait" was a term shared with students at the opening lecture. Not surprisingly, this seventh objective was the one the students said they encountered the most. For example, members of the Gifted and Talented group were in an almost constant state of frustration. It was not until their third recruitment drive in the second-to-last week of class that they generated their interview sample, allowing resolution of the project.

The class officially met twice a week, first for a two-hour lecture and then a one-hour tutorial. Formal lectures were few and the class was quite impromptu. The two-hour class always began with a verbal class report from each group. The group but most importantly three was required to stand in front of the class and provide an update on their progress. This was in line with Hauhart and Grahe's recommendations to organise regular instructor–student meetings and to encourage peer review during class meeting discussions.

Although the reports were only a few minutes long, the discussions that followed could be extended to 10–15 minutes as the issues raised were usually about getting in and getting along in the research process or about problems with collection techniques or analysis. Over the years, locating inadequacies in the students' previous learning has led to revisions of the year two research methods course, inclusive of new teaching units on techniques on how to recruit and interview participants.

The second scheduled weekly class, the tutorial, was made an optional part of the course where students would come by my office during these times to discuss specific problems they were having. In various parts of this book, I describe this teaching technique as more coaching or supported mentoring. Contact between students and myself is established in the first lecture. Students are given my home phone number and told they can contact me at *any time* if their project loses shape, if their liaison person is unhappy with the group or if their personal safety is in jeopardy. Students are advised not to use the number for less immediate concerns like requesting an assignment extension. A feature of all evaluations over the years either conducted by me as a part of my ongoing research or officially by the university have commented on my ever-presence on email. The expectation is that I respond immediately to all emails. Additionally, students will come to my office outside office hours to share their excitement or frustrations.

The student experience

In 2012 and 2013, I received a University of Otago learning and teaching research grant to evaluate both my students and the community liaison members. Results from the community liaison members are reported in Chapter 5. What follows is how my students explain the course to a research assistant both during and after the course by answering a comparative "job interview" question:

> *Tell me about the research design of a project you were involved in, its outcomes, and explain what your contribution was to the project.*

The answers to this question were integral to assessing the independent research project recorded both at the start and completion of the course, allowing two evaluations. First, how well does the research methods course taught in year two prepare students for this interview question? Second, at the end of the course, how well does the course enhance their research skills and confidence to answer the question?

The question proved a useful measurement tool and the answers at the end of the course were qualitatively different when compared with the opening responses; many of these initial responses were answered in seconds rather than minutes. Other questions asked by a research assistant employed to run both the focus groups with students held mid-semester and the one-on-one interviews held at the end of the semester asked thematic questions about their confidence in public speaking, ability to work in teams and the outputs of their research, as well as their reflections on the course.

At the end of the course, when the students had completed their projects and had received their grades, the research assistant and I conducted the final interviews mostly by telephone, although one occurred opportunistically face to face with two students. These interviews asked students to reflect broadly on their experiences but also specifically invited them to answer the job interview question. All interviews and the focus groups were transcribed and thematically analysed using both inductive approaches to draw out and to exemplify common themes of interest.

Results are presented here as themes of interest explored throughout the course, via initial individual interviews (ii), focus groups (fg), group presentations (gp) and final individual interviews (fi). In the text below, each of the themes is described and illustrated using quotations under student pseudonyms. The themes are:

- confidence as a sociologist-researcher
- public speaking

- teamwork
- producing sociology outputs
- the job interview question.

An assumption underpinning *the research question* sought some indication that the students' participation in the course resulted in some increase in confidence in their ability to articulate sociology with some fluency. This fluency stemmed from participating in the project but also from the course pedagogy, which required students to engage in routine public speaking in the weekly class meeting. As with the initial meeting with the community liaison, this public speaking was not part of the four-part research project. These verbal reports also functioned as a peer review among the students. Team members were required to take turns in updating other students about their project's progress and how they were addressing any real or potential roadblocks in their research. This "learning by doing" was the source of most of the classroom discussion throughout the semester.

On research confidence

At the start of the course, Melinda (a pseudonym) exemplified the lack of confidence about undertaking a research project and "being" a sociologist, as expressed by many of the students:

> Usually you can like do a project and then kind of like forget about it, but this is more realistic, and you have more invested into what you're doing. You have to like build up the basic knowledge on your topic which you haven't really heard of before, and then you have to go out there and like talk to the actual people who run it, or the people who use it. And try to sound like, well not try to sound like, but have some sort of like authority. Whereas I don't feel like I do.
>
> (Melinda, ii)

After the course, students presented radically different expressions of self-efficacy from those at the start:

> I learnt a lot … like how things work … I didn't really know the processes … involved … I think that I'd be better at it now that I know.
>
> (Kelly, fi)

> I've learnt heaps of research skills, interviewing, knowing what it's like being interviewed, thematic analysis, writing up; really cool.
>
> (Charlotte, fi)

It was really valuable having you [the lecturer] there to tell us what you do, but I feel if I conducted another one I know what to do now.

(Jenny, fi)

On public speaking

Public speaking was integral to all stages of the course as well as in the final group presentation to members of the community, and this loomed as a source of significant anxiety for the students. Brendan's response is typical of these initial concerns:

I feel like I'm mostly in my comfort zone but the only thing I do have a problem with is talking in front of a lot of people. If I'm talking with one person personally, yeah, I don't really have any issues at all, but when it's in front of a group of people.

(Brendan, ii)

Given that those students who were majoring in Sociology had to this point not been required to present their research, this was a significant concern:

I'm not a massive public speaker, and [the lecturer] tends to throw that out there: everyone just stand up and just tell us about your group. And my group is more silent than I am. So it is usually me who's going to be speaking. I get real nervous.

(Catherine, ii)

Midway through the course, for the many still without a clearly formulated research project, anxieties about public speaking had not subsided. The focus group voices reported:

I hate public speaking.

(Melinda)

I'm not the best public speaker.

(Catherine)

Remarkably, in their final interviews, none of the students mentioned this anxiety. Students described their toughest challenges but none mentioned their fear of public speaking. It appears that public speaking, and its challenges, became part of the job for these students.

On teamwork

Given that many entry-level policy-analyst positions involve working in team environments, a key research question examined the extent to which students, particularly those new to teamwork at a tertiary level, are able to negotiate the various challenges that teamwork involves. Therefore, a question the students were asked in their initial interview related to their past experience of teamwork. For many of the students, it was the first time in their university career that they had worked in teams (particularly in the case of Sociology major students). A few had prior experience:

> I'm always really sceptical about group work because I've worked in so many groups and it's just been like people don't show up or they don't pull their weight, and that's just irritating. But I think this might be a bit different because the groups are smaller and because you're kind of, you have to rely on everybody else. So hopefully that will be fine.
>
> (Georgina, ii)

The focus groups illustrated the perhaps unanticipated enjoyment of working closely with fellow students on a research project. Charlotte and Ruth were quick to point out the benefits of this working arrangement in terms of what each individual could bring to the research process:

> I think we're lucky in our group that we all do have different strengths. It probably doesn't work that way in some groups, but it's like we didn't really have to talk about it, it just, we just figured out what each other was going to do, and then just did it.
>
> (Charlotte, fg)

> It's good that we get to share the load. I've never worked in a group before either. Yeah, and because we get to refine each other's ideas and help each other out, yeah.
>
> (Ruth, ii)

The final individual interviews largely confirmed our mid-term results. Teams, by and large, operated very successfully:

> It's really valuable working in a small team where everyone had different strengths.
>
> (Melinda, fi)

> I had a great team and we were all interested in education so we were all invested in making a good assessment. We wanted to get an A and we were determined that we were going to deserve it.
>
> (Catherine, fi)

And different teams organically found different ways to get together:

> We set up a Facebook group to talk things through.
>
> (Georgina, fi)

Nevertheless, these students' enthusiasm for working in groups was not unreserved:

> It's [the course] been a kind of good experience because I learned how to work in a group .... But it takes more time to do things in a group than alone.
>
> (Emily, fi)

> I liked the teamwork, makes things easier, shared workload, couldn't have done this on my own but it was also the most challenging ... working in a team.
>
> (Brendan, fi)

A challenge I had not predicted was the that posed by teamwork. One group in 2012 had too many leaders and needed mediation twice during the course to defuse tensions. Another group had no leaders and their project floundered. At the initial meeting with their community liaison, the group arrived with blank notebooks ready to write down what the "teacher" said. In subsequent years, these initial meetings were role-played in class as this interaction was not intuitive. However, even with these role-plays, some students found the interaction cumbersome. Other groups by this stage had completed a literature review and produced tentative research questions. In hindsight, these problems may have been the result of the course's teething problems as these types of teamwork issues have not been an issue again. Additionally, in the following years, more attention was given to professional development on how to interact with the groups the students were assigned to.

On producing sociology outputs

Students understood from an early stage that they were to produce a final written report on their project or create a video for their group. At first, this task was overwhelming:

I'd be quite nervous about the actual final outcome, because we are making some sort of video or something to show to the public.

(Jane, ii)

But by the end of the course, these concerns re-emerged largely as a sense of pride in what was achieved:

and at the end of it all we gathered all the information and we wrote what was going to be a newspaper article on what it is like to be a newspaper deliverer and in that article we focused on the themes of safety, delivering heavy papers, bad weather. How it didn't actually turn out to be an isolated job at all, how there was lots of social interaction and it was really cool at the end to see the progress we made from being given a topic we knew nothing about to writing an article which was quite detailed about a job none of us really considered before.

(Melinda, fg)

On the virtues of experiential learning

At the end of the course, and once the final grades had been submitted, I asked some students how they would describe the course to another student thinking of enrolling in a future class. Here, the answers illuminate the ownership of the course content but also that this class was different from others, less abstract and required a greater commitment:

I think I would probably say to the student that it is the most valuable course you could do at Uni because it is practical … and it's really valuable working in a small team where everyone had different strengths.

(Melinda, fi)

I would say even if there was a bit more time put into it, it was time that you didn't mind, I didn't mind putting in the time for it because it was interesting and it was real.

(Charlotte, fi)

It also became clear that the students found this "realness" enabled them to "own" their research projects:

Like it's one thing to kind of apply them [theories] to something that's hypothetical but when you've got to apply them to something that's real and in front of you and actually has a lot of variables you can't control that's quite a big learning curve to realise that there's a lot of things you can't control, and when they happen they happen.

(Jane, gp)

On responding to the job interview question

In general, and particularly in response to the job interview question, the students demonstrated a profound empathy with the discipline, its methodological approaches and its problems. The following captures a process of development:

> I think if I was to go into a job interview now I would be able to tell them that I had done a research project from the beginning to the end and when we first got our research topic we had absolutely no idea what we were going to do, we didn't even really have a project, we just had a theme and then you find a question and find some things you want to figure out and then you can write some questions and ask how is the best way we can do this?

(Melinda, fi)

Partway through the process, some students were developing considerable confidence to describe an unfolding journey in response to the interview question:

> First of all we decided we needed to learn more about newspaper delivering so we did some research with a literature review and then we didn't really have a research question but we had aims that we wanted to find out what sort of things happen in newspaper delivery, what the job entails and what the best and worst aspects were. So we wrote down some questions which involved things like what do in a mornings work? What are the best parts of the job? What are the hardest things? Why did you decide to become a newspaper deliverer? And then we were able to get some newspaper delivering people and talked to them and interviewed them one on one and then we talked to the manager of the newspaper and they also gave us some more names and they had a few things that they wanted to find out and then we interviewed more people … at the end of every interview you would stop and say what was good in this? And we started coding our work and finding different themes and see how those themes related to our initial thoughts and initial aims of the project.

(Melinda, fg)

Final interviews demonstrated a range of abilities to respond to the job interview question, and most contrasted the course with normal research methods courses. Simon spoke well in response to the job interview question:

> I worked in a group on the Dunedin Book Bus project and we did qualitative field research and had regular meetings with both the manager, the bus driver and the people that visit the Book Bus. Obviously we would liaise with [the lecturer] as well, coming up with and designing the research itself. We then answered the research question by making a video for the library that could be used for public use. I would maybe tell them about what the video was like and maybe go through the process that we used like starting with observation and interviewing the manager then coming up with themes from there and then using the readings you have given us for coding and stuff like that. Depending on how in-depth they wanted me to go I'd tell them all about it if I could. Like we also got an understanding of things like ethics and how to interview whereas in the methods classes we just got given the transcripts of interviews and stuff. In this paper you are conducting the interviews and yeah.

(Simon, fi)

These outcomes varied. Some responses were poorly structured. Some were adequately descriptive but lacked enthusiasm. There was not a clear link between the quality of the outcomes of individual projects and the nature of student responses to the job interview question.

My own reflections on these first heady days of the course were mainly positive and reflective. Any negative learnings from the first course, detailed in the next chapter, came from interviewing a member of each of the five community groups. From the students, I had the chance to evaluate my initial aspiration, to create pathways to employment for students. I had been concerned about the prospects and abilities of Sociology graduates to secure employment in related fields, but this research engendered a substantial sense of pride in what students had achieved and what I had facilitated. An unexpected outcome of the course was the quality of letters of recommendation I was able to write for many of these students seeking their first job. In the past, my letters of recommendation were limited as I often strained to recall whether the student had made verbal contributions and, as a rule, I relied on course records to locate their letter grade achievement for assignments and the course.

A lightbulb moment appeared serendipitously when I wrote letters of recommendation for these students at the end of each year. The letters usually delivered to employers over the phone, were *thick descriptions* of their projects and progress and, most importantly, the courage they demonstrated in getting through the various stages of the task: meeting the community liaison, developing research questions, writing a literature review, constructing a research instrument, gathering and analysing data, writing the final report and presenting it to members of the community. Additionally, the course allowed me to comment with some authority on the students' ability to work within a team.

All students were encouraged to put my name down as a reference, but prior to them submitting their employment application, I asked them to contact me out of courtesy. On these occasions, I would ask them to email me the letter they wrote to the employer. In some circumstances, I proofread the letter and suggested ways they could promote themselves in a more favourable light to a future employer. I also made myself available for mock job interviews. Invariably I would ask two questions:

1   Tell me about yourself?
2   Tell me about the job that you are applying for and what skills do you take to the job?

I usually tape-recorded these interviews and gave the student the only copy for them to re-listen and to take on board any suggestions I had made for elaborating their answers.

Over the semester, I had seen the students' confidence grow incrementally during their projects' weekly updates to other students. While at first the students reported how daunting speaking in front of the class or meeting the community liaison was, it was not long before other roadblocks superseded these fears; for instance, would research participants respond to the students' requests for them to be interviewed? In time, each of these fears was met and overcome with support.

Over scaffolding

One personal disappointment in the interviews and focus groups presented above was how rarely the students in the first year of the course mentioned their interaction with the community liaison. In hindsight, this omission is due to the structuring of the course. The imagery I want to share is of a house with scaffolding in preparation of painting. The image is of an abundance of scaffolding in which the house is masked—it is not visible. In 2012, my best intentions masked the students. For example, gaining ethics approval ahead of time was sensible—I did not want delays from the ethics committees to impact the students' projects—but in doing so it robbed the students of some important embryonic micro research moments.

Due to the structure of a 25-page high-risk ethics application submitted to a full ethics committee, many facets of the research design of the students' projects, if not all, were established at the outset. These facets included:

- The projects' titles
- The justification or benefit of the research
- Some reference to a literature review
- The research question or problem
- The intended methodology
- If a survey was involved, a completed questionnaire
- Indigenous consultation
- The likely output (video, written report)
- Most importantly, all of the above were negotiated with these groups prior to the students enrolling in the course.

Writing an ethics application on behalf of the students robbed them of the ability to take responsibility for the formation of their project as an involved process. These responsibilities included meeting with each of the community groups to negotiate and establish the research question and decide on a suitable research output. Yet the "moment" was more basic than simply a meeting. *Basic* involved arranging a time and place to meet the community liaison plus the swapping of recognition tropes. One infamous learning occurred in a Starbucks, when the students sat waiting at a table adjacent to the table that the community member was sitting at for 30 minutes. Basic not only involved learning what project the community liaison wanted researched; these liaison officers often wanted to know how the course was organised and its assessment, and the students were required to be ambassadors and explain themselves and what this Public Sociology course was all about.

The next chapter provides accounts from these community liaisons who thought that I was too hands-on. The facets above are illustrative of that. I did too much and the community groups thought so too. They wanted to meet the students more often, not less. My initial sense was well intentioned; not wanting to burden the community groups or over-burden (with time delays) the students but finding my actions not appreciated or not constructive was an uncomfortable lesson.

In future iterations of the course, I would no longer complete the students' ethics applications before the commencement of the course, and instead students would be responsible for completing a low-risk application, which would only require approval from the Head of Department instead of the

University Ethics Committee. To expedite this ethics review process away from a 25-page document with full committee review to a 4–5-page Head of Department sign-off, I manipulated these student projects by making them less 'risky.' For example, I prohibited children under 16 (the age of consent in New Zealand) from being interviewed, as gaining parental consent would have delayed the onset of the project.

In sum, there are two findings from this research evaluation of the 2012 students. The students did benefit from the experiential learning; they did encounter real research participants and a variety of seemingly insurmountable roadblocks. The learning outcome was positive; a surge in confidence in public speaking and knowledge of what the component parts of any sociology research project were. The four stages of the course provided incremental and manageable growth steps. The students' ability to articulate an answer to the job interview question was enhanced by the end of the course, though this remained variable. Surprisingly, the ability to write (or speak to on the phone) a job recommendation for these students was greatly enhanced by the degree that I was involved in each of the student projects and their false starts.

The second finding the evaluation revealed as a recommendation for the future iterations of this course was my involvement in the construction of the ethics application prior to the class beginning. This well-intentioned act made me too hands-on, virtually stage-managing the relationship between the community liaison and the students. This was not an ideal learning outcome. In subsequent years, ethics applications would be written within the semester and after the students and the community liaisons had decided on a research question and a research output. In fact, in future years there will be room for the students to choose their own research topics. These choices were both a strength and a challenge to be faced in future years.

Note

1 This chapter draws in part from an article written by Tolich, M., Paris, A. & Shephard, K. (2014). An evaluation of experiential learning in a sociology internship class. *New Zealand Sociology*, 29(1), 119–134. Permission has been granted by the journal and authors.

5 Overreaching community organisations

By the end of 2012, the benefits of the Public Sociology course for the students had been established, though there was room for improvement. I then asked the five community liaisons (the managers of the Book Bus, the newspaper, the food banks, the gifted and talented programme and the indigenous outreach (Science Wananga)) if they saw benefits from participating in the Public Sociology course. What was their experience of interacting with the students and with me? Of the two studies following the 2012 course (the students and the community liaisons experience), listening to the honest and robust accounts by community liaisons provided some of the most excruciating moments in my teaching career. If this chapter is the omelette, I was the eggs. As this chapter attests,[1] I may have been well intentioned, but I made mistakes. Luckily, once identified, they were remedied.

The original goal for getting the opinions of the community liaisons was a pragmatic interest in the sustainability of this outreach, allowing my students to revisit these groups year after year. My fear was Dunedin's isolation and small population of 100,000, 25,000 of whom leave town at the end of the academic year. Dunedin is not Wellington, with a myriad of government departments, or Auckland, with its 1.5 million people. Interviewing the five liaison members was designed to locate problems in their relationship with the course and address them, allowing future students to be welcomed back. This chapter begins by briefly addressing sustainability but quickly morphs into a useful critical analysis of the course from intelligent, independent and dispassionate people. What they said transformed the course and many of my initial assumptions about community involvement in university projects.

Sustainable Public Sociology

An early assumption made of these five projects was that there were few community groups in an isolated city and that there was a need to recycle these groups in subsequent years. This assumption was valid, but it proved overly cautious. It also overlooked that all of these community groups had worked with students in various capacities previously. Thus, on the basis of prior experience, community project managers generally wanted clear lines of communication and clear planning, and for this I failed to deliver.

The Marine Science Manager had experienced some good past outcomes with interns from the university, but some of the past students and their teachers, who had over promised and under delivered, had disappointed. Factors contributing to this were the university teachers not being adequately involved in the outreach. The Marine Science Manager was close to giving up on interns:

> The academic requirements are what drives the students, so if they don't match expectations, then there is potential for disappointment. They're nice people. And they try hard, and it's often not their fault the project does not get finished, so you end up writing a reference letter. I'm just about to give up with [university] students because I've done it for years and I'm often dissatisfied.

The Dunedin City Libraries' Mobile Library (the Book Bus) Manager also had had less-than-satisfactory prior experiences when assisting tertiary students. She said it was difficult sometimes to make up work for placement-type students.

> It's pointless, you know, you have to make up your task and … it's a waste of time.

The Book Bus Manager was clear in what research she did not want. Anything that would harm her programme was a threat. In her first interview, she came close to discussing an embargo on results likely to harm the programme. She also did not want another quantitative description of book usage, but stories from people who valued the Book Bus:

> [The Book Bus] doesn't make money, it's only a social good … so you are constantly feeling like you're on the budget line. You are always saying we are a good, we are a good … We have no budget to promote ourselves.

Against these hopes and expectations for the mode of operation, I had in mind the needs of the students embarking on an experiential, and therefore inevitably somewhat unstructured, programme of learning. For example, my goal of relying on the students to communicate directly with the community managers was supposedly to create independence, autonomy and responsibility. Those involved sought a balance between these opposing objectives that developed differently in each setting and yielded different perspectives of functionality.

The community managers generally also wanted applied outcomes, often of a particular nature. "Applied outcomes" can be characterised as the community wanting fresh eyes; an independent evaluation of their programmes as befits the sociologist researchers in their midst. The Social Welfare Service Manager, for example, wanted fresh eyes, which she characterised as external persons justifying the worth of their programmes to outsiders. The manager lamented that they were providing food to the same people without much social change:

> I sometimes find a fresh approach or a new approach looking at it, because we have our own perspectives, but the students having a look at it can always offer something different.

This not-for-profit Social Welfare Service Manager also saw her involvement in the course as an extension of service, this time for the student researchers. The Science Wananga Manager saw the course as a unique opportunity:

> Something I have wanted to do for a while and having the internship group on board has kind of made it happen.

She saw the students' report, justifying the project to other people, and she was genuinely interested in what the students would come up with. The newspaper's circulation manager was more prescriptive, wanting feedback specifically on the training and the training booklet given to Dawn Patrol newspaper deliverers.

Ideally, the students' outputs should have closely matched both the form and content of the actual needs of each community project, but everyday academic language exposed discrepant core assumptions. For example, characterising the students' relationship with the community manager as a "client relationship" jarred sensibilities.

The Book Bus Manager, for example, did not see herself as a client as she was not paying for the service. She saw herself as more of a person who may receive some benefit, and saw the project as potentially having value of a specific nature:

> Anything I get I will be happy with. It's been ten years and I always thought I would like a video to show people about what we do.

What this manager wanted was for the students to provide evidence that their service was relevant to the community and to demonstrate buyer interviews with customers that the Book Bus library made a difference in these people's lives.

This revelation provided a lightbulb insight into the goals of most of the community groups my students researched. The organisations were not well resourced, and they wanted to know, were they relevant? And, did they make a difference?

These interviews with managers also divulged what the managers wanted from me. In short, these five community managers required more clarity on the objectives of the project (academic and applied), a time frame for the work to be completed, an outline of the resources (including peoples' time) required and an agreed process for communication between all parties. Against this, I should have been obliged to better communicate the experiential nature of the research course and the limitations to the organisation that this implied.

Effective and ongoing communication

The errors I made were not novel. The service learning literature contains examples of where community partners have felt exploited by service learning programmes (Tryon & Stoecker, 2008). I was mindful of numerous pitfalls and I attempted to ensure that the key problem areas defined by Tryon and Stoecker (2008) were avoided. These authors suggest that the "success of a service-learning project depends on the level of commitment made by the academic and community partners, the effectiveness of communication, and the compatibility of the service-learning program and the student to the community organization's goals" (Tryon & Stoecker, 2008, 56).

An outcome of this interview with the managers found that the community need for communication was not uniform. The Marine Sciences Manager wanted me to be more involved when she met the students. The Science Wananga Manager, on the other hand, wanted more contact with the students. The Social Welfare Service Manager anticipated and achieved substantial autonomy by the students. After the initial meeting, where she shared a vision for the project plan that the students compare and contrast four Dunedin food banks, she had little contact with the students until the final report was delivered, but she did delegate her front-line staff to engage with the students.

Failure to realise that different expectations are adequately communicated about the needs of each project group created diverse outcomes. I did not always understand what the community managers needed or how extensively they wanted to be involved in the research.

The Book Bus

The Book Bus Manager loved the YouTube video and showed the film to the city council at the Central Library's annual Christmas party. The students were invited. Nonetheless, the librarian found the whole research process uncertain:

> [The three-minute video] expressed the Book Bus values without being dollars and cents or numbers of people and books. We [already] know the Book Bus numbers are declining, and the central library usage is up, more to do with access to wi-fi than borrowing books. We want stories about how visiting the Book Bus was the only time someone talked to him that week. [The three-minute video] gives us a higher profile because we are a little, forgotten library in a sense …. I'm thinking I might take [the three-minute video] out with me to rest homes.

Mistakes the students made and the absence of my involvement overshadowed a positive outcome. For example, the students showed inexperience by attempting to interview the manager about the Book Bus's mission statement on their first meeting. The manager said:

> I can't do [an interview] while serving customers. But later we met in my office and had an hour-long chat. So that was a learning occasion for the students. They were keen and interested.

Upon learning about this error and using a learning-by-doing pedagogy, I devoted more class time in the next years to discussing how to get into a research site and get along in it. This was part of the professional development that is a major part of the teaching for this course.

In her post-research interview, the Book Bus Manager revealed further miscommunication. Mid-way through the 12-week course, she began to feel uncertainty about how the three-minute video would be produced. Progress had been slow. At one stage the students had moved from observing the Book Bus customers to interviewing them, but the manager did not know this. Responsibility seemed to be hers. She asked, was it up to her to "dish them up on a plate?" This was the same as the students who turned up to the Science Wananga Manager with blank pieces of paper, wanting her to outline the course of their project.

As the project progressed, I was unaware that the responsibility for recruitment of research subjects remained a point of contention. Even though the project turned out positively for all parties, the last few days of the project were frenetic and heavily reliant on the community manager's resources and goodwill. For example, the videotaping of the customer interviews took place over two hectic days in less than ideal conditions. The wind noise recorded detracted from the quality of the output.

Always positive, the Book Bus Manager said that next time, the students should give a "wee bit" more notice. This message, although directed at the students, is my responsibility as the lecturer. As for the presentation of the video, she said:

> I love it, I love it ... I've never really been outside the bus and watched it. Seen how pretty it is, how nice it is, and it was just really heart-warming actually to hear some of the people get quite passionate about it because we don't talk like that on the bus.

Without her assistance, this video project would not have succeeded, but it did, and a great deal of credit is given to her for seeing potential for the video. It is noteworthy that the students' video is no longer on the Dunedin library's website in the form that the students created. The basic structure of the visual content of the video remains, but the Book Bus Manager has deleted the soundtrack and replaced it with a more updated version (*Dunedin Public Libraries – Bookbus Service*, n.d.).

Marine Science outreach

The Marine Science Manager saw clear benefits for the students:

> I think they enjoyed the fact that they actually got some real data and it was something that was really useful to us, so you know, I think they got real-life experience in doing a research project.

In her interview, this community manager scaled back her initial aspirations of a publishable journal article. The students she saw were hard working, their involvement going beyond the minimum; they attended and observed university students involved in the 2012 Gifted and Talented programme giving their research presentations to their parents, and they wanted to know more about the programme that they were doing research on. They were professional in the way that they conducted themselves and were really interested in the project. All the students involved in this project had chosen to work on the project, and all had further career interests in the education field. Although they did not develop anything close to a publishable paper, the research techniques (telephone interviews) and the typed interview transcripts provided useful insight into the program.

> I wanted to get something out of it and we will, we probably can incorporate some of the data into articles that we write.

The main benefit that the Marine Science Manager got from the project was not from the final report but from the discussion she had with the three students and from gaining further insight into the Gifted and Talented students' experience of the programme.

A positive expectation of the course went unrealised for the Marine Science Manager. She expected more involvement from me and was pleased to be part of the evaluative research on this course. However, she expected it to be more of an action research framework where she would be able to feed back into the research process. The initial meeting between the Marine Science Manager and the students did not involve me, and she saw this as an error. In my defence, I saw this initial meeting as promoting the students' autonomy and them taking control. The Marine Science Manager saw this differently:

> I think it was fine for course controller not to be there yesterday, but I think he needs to be there at other meetings. Because I don't want him meeting with them and deciding the research should go in a different direction and doing this, and then me thinking it's going this way—that not what I expected.

The Marine Science Manager is correct; I should have been present at the initial meeting. In subsequent years, I was present more than not. However, in 2017 I stopped attending these meetings unless my students requested my presence. None did. By 2017 I felt confident that I knew the nuances of this course. I also felt my students could articulate the course for their community liaison.

In 2012, my plan that students take responsibility for the project was not always realistic for third-year students and my learning objectives required more development, and this was forthcoming following this dialogue between parties. Disappointments would have been avoidable had there been better ongoing communication between the course co-ordinator and the Marine Science Manager. An example of a missed opportunity was in the creation of the students' literature review. The students' 3000-word article began in a confessional style, highlighting the importance of the tall poppy syndrome predicted by the literature. Had the Marine Sciences Manager been involved in the development and critique of the literature review the research project may have had a different emphasis. I regret this and take responsibility for it.

Social service outreach

The Social Welfare Service Manager responded very positively to both the written and the private oral presentation the students gave her:

I am very happy with what they came up with. [W]e anecdotally had an idea of what we all do and our criteria but it is a really useful document to have well written up and researched because it has come directly from the frontline workers in each food bank and their perception of how their services are run and we are all really different. And then what happened was the students pulled it together and did their own analysis.

The Social Welfare Service Manager quickly put the report written by the students working with her to use:

I used it to give a talk about a week after I got the report I had to go down to the Centre of Innovation who were doing a big promo day on food and food sustainability … it was really wonderful to have that accessible information which is so up to date.

As outsiders, the students provided the Social Welfare Service Manager with fresh eyes and the manager saw the project as useful and would use interns again.

These three managers had a positive experience with the course. However, the most important learning for me came from the other two sites that were not, in other respects, as successful.

The newspaper deliverers

Two newspaper circulation managers interviewed at both the beginning and the end of the project said in the post-project interviews that the students' 3000-word written report was not what they had expected. A series of 500-word reports on various topics could have had more utility. The managers read the 3000-word paper more like a set of stories or a novel. When one of the two managers mentioned the word novel, the other one said, "That's what I was trying to put my finger on!"

The managers also took issue with the content of the article, specifically the discussion of the unsmiling face image the newspaper circulation managers used to inform the newspaper delivery person that a customer had made a complaint. The students' article reported that the deliverers did not know exactly what this frowning face meant. However, to the managers, the meaning was clearly defined in the training booklet given to all newspaper deliverers.

[The image] has nothing to do with wet papers or anything like that [the students] wrote the articles on the kids who had no idea which hasn't reflected well on us.

As the interview with the managers progressed, the managers did see some merit in the 3000-word article:

> reading between the lines in the article you can actually say, hang on maybe the kids aren't reading the [training] books well enough and maybe we could change our training a bit more, maybe do refreshers and—We know we are behind on that. That was definitely one of the things I picked up on.

Would the newspaper do it again? The circulation manager was not convinced:

> That's a tricky one. I think we would have to have clearer objectives about what we were supposed to get back.

The students' response to this critique was to write a 500-word paper focusing solely on how the newspaper deliverers could create a safety plan for themselves by virtue of getting to know early rising customers on their route. This output was presented to the newspaper after the final grades had been submitted. Thus, none of these students received additional credit for this additional work.

In 2012, this post-course effort, after the grades were assigned, was a one-off. In 2013 it would become more common and by 2014 it was the rule. By then the students had become hooked into the goals in their organisation and finishing the project well for them was imperative.

The Science Wananga

Communication in all five projects did not proceed perfectly, but specific reflection on the missing communication in the Science Wananga project provides the greatest learning for me. There was a genuine confusion of responsibility of roles in this particular project between me, the community manager and the students. The Science Wananga Manager's expectations were never met, as she wanted to be involved in each stage of the project.

In the beginning, the Science Wananga Manager had a sense that the students, she and I were a research team. To that end, she provided the research team with an existing interview she had conducted with a research subject and the names of five persons likely to be willing to take part in an interview. She also expressed her willingness to meet regularly with the students. However, as the project unfolded the research team did not manage to meet to discuss the production of the information sheet or the types of questions they would ask.

The Science Wananga Manager was disappointed in the overall outcome. She saw the students' final report as having little worth, being filled with inaccuracies and potentially harming the reputation of the programme. There was also a loss of trust and unrealised expectations:

> I stand here with no useful data or the transcripts. My sadness is that I've wasted a lot of time with this process and not got anything out of it.

To some extent, the community manager found fault in particular with me, and this was a fair assessment. Unlike other managers who wanted more involvement with me, the Science Wananga Manager saw me as too involved in mediating between the community manager and the students:

> I think the fact that the lecturer was very much mediating in the middle actually distanced the possibility of any relationship between me and the students.

However, both this manager and I noted that the project was more culturally sensitive than other projects in this course. Indeed, the community manager pointed out that I had questioned the suitability of the topic for *these* students:

> [The lecturer] obviously felt that students maybe weren't particularly engaged with this type of topic of kaupapa or process so that is maybe something to think about; who is selected for which project.

Like other student groups, the Science Wananga group met with their community manager at the end of the project to give a verbal report of the already-delivered written report. This was only the second time that the community manager and students had met, the first being the inaugural meeting to discuss the nature of the project. This was the meeting where the students arrived with blank pieces of paper rather than some initial ideas. Thus, without ongoing dialogue, trust had not developed. Before the second meeting, the students said they were nervous discussing their report. One student's report of the final meeting with their manager saw it as a tense "flat meeting." They felt they had underperformed.

In sum, at one level, the number of lightbulb moments that appear in this chapter reveal intense moments of learning.

- Communication between the community managers and I needed to be in-depth, ongoing and nuanced.
- Expectations of outcome and process needed to be concrete and agreed.
- Community liaisons are likely to be active rather than passive. Having signed up for the project, they are most likely to want to be involved in all aspects of the research. To promote this active involvement, they should be sent the literature review, the information sheet and the interview questions for comment as they are generated and before they are sent to interviewees.
- Community liaisons should be informed of the course schedules, milestones that the students must meet and the marking criteria, as this is what is driving the students' involvement and will help the community manager set aside the time and resources for the students at the appropriate time.
- The students and I should discuss in advance with the community manager how the final report will be presented.

The experiences described in this chapter suggest that the benefits to community organisations are complex. They may depend on clear expectations and lines of communication between, and among, involved parties. But they also may be influenced by and dependent on the intervention of happenstance in contributing to the experiences of those involved. As with many educational endeavours of consequence, balance is important. In the following years, I endeavoured not to make these mistakes again. This did not stop me from making other mistakes.

Note

1 This chapter draws in part from an article written by Tolich, M., Shephard, K., Carson, S. & Hunt, D. (2013), Co-managing the sustainability of University internship programmes in brownfield sites. *New Zealand Sociology*, 28(1), 156–171. Permission has been granted by the journal and the authors.

6   Fostering student responsibility for others

In 2013, I changed the course markedly. In 2012, before the course commenced, I had spoken with the five community liaisons, planned the research projects and wrote ethics applications for each, outlining the entire project, including indicative interview questions. In 2013, I was more hands-off. The 25-page ethics application for each project had been overkill; it required that the research question be stated and the research instrument (such as a survey or an unstructured interview guide) be designated in advance. All of these tasks could be done by the students themselves. Moreover, the ethics application form required a precise research output. I had made too many command decisions, such as whether the output should be a pamphlet, a poster, a video recording or a written report. It was no wonder the organisations' managers were displeased with my personal role. Preplanning had been deemed essential as it was anticipated that the ethics application could take some weeks to process, and avoidance of any delay was seen as important. In the second year, I no longer found I needed to do most of this preparatory groundwork as the projects were ethically not high risk. Moreover, the ethics application participant information sheet became the students' primary responsibility, and with it a door to many other responsibilities that the students were ready to open.[1]

In 2013, the course enrolment remained manageable for an experimental course. Fifteen students were enrolled, the same number as in 2012. Each was invited to take part in an ongoing evaluation of the course with a guarantee that if they did not take part, it would make no difference to their course or grade. Taking part in the evaluation involved being available for interviews at the end of the course. Ten students volunteered to do so. Students had the option of being interviewed by the research assistant either by themselves or within their groups of three. At least one member was interviewed from each of the six groups and for three of the groups all members were interviewed.

All interviews were subsequently transcribed and thematically analysed to draw out and exemplify common themes of interest that arose from within the interview. Overall, many of the themes the students expressed (such as the uniqueness of the course) were similar to those found in the study of the 2012 students and therefore are not reported here. However, the major finding in 2013 stemmed from the removal of the ethics application scaffolding. In general, the students responded positively and in the transcribed interviews described a sense of themselves being more involved in the project from start to finish.

The 2013 students did not report any problems in writing the ethics participant information sheet for their organisation or any burden stemming from negotiating the research design. They did say that their initial meeting with the community liaison was stressful, but this tended to be a momentary glitch and the students had little trouble writing a research protocol inclusive of a literature review, an outline of the research problem and the rationale for choosing the methodology (i.e. survey, interview guide).

The research assistant also interviewed me in 2013 after interviewing the students, as all of the students reflected a great deal on the impact of what some described as my "mentoring" role. A notable feature in 2013 was that some of the students continued to work on their projects even after they had been submitted for a grade. This reflected an emergent form of responsibility that transformed the students' projects and the course itself. In 2014, the students again responded enthusiastically to the removal of the scaffolding, which allowed them to take more initiative towards conceiving the research project and developing the research design.

Students meeting the community liaison 2013

The meeting of the designated community member "cold" by the groups of three students, without knowing the scope of the research project the liaison person had in mind, produced some initial problems for the students. Most found this meeting a "nerve-racking" encounter, compounded by the fact that this was the students' first experience where they themselves had to conceive of their own research question. Even though most of them had carried out a cursory background review about the organisation by the first meeting, most students expected the community liaison to frame the project even to the point of stipulating the output, be it a written report, a pamphlet or a video. For example, the Wriggle and Rhyme group were researching a parents and babies music group that met weekly in the city library. Not only were the students nervous at the first meeting, but this continued when they first met the participants and their wriggling babies. The three students were overwhelmed when faced with 40 young mothers and their babies en masse for the first time; one student described it in her journal as "really intimidating," and she asked herself why she was invading their space.

It's just sort of really intimidating when there's all these sorts of mothers there wondering what you're doing their space kind of thing and just worried that they aren't going to want to talk to us and help us out so

Meeting community liaisons and participants continued to be anxiety-producing but the Wriggle and Rhyme students overcame their fears and anxieties.

I think it's changed us as people, like I'm a lot more confident in myself because it was a hard task to overcome, especially when you're not exactly outgoing before you do it.

In hindsight, this issue could have been better addressed to some extent and in 2014, these initial meetings were rehearsed in role-plays during class.

A second emergent responsibility evident in 2013 was that all of the groups went beyond the requirements of the paper for their final outputs.

This was one of the two major turning points in the course. After students had completed their last assignment and exam, they maintained contact with the community organisations they had been working with to continue their work or put significant finishing touches on their projects. The reasons they gave for this emergent work ethic were similar: members of the Wriggle and Rhyme Group thought that the relationships they had built were important.

I feel like we've built up relationships you can't just chuck out, like you have to keep in contact with them, yeah, because otherwise it would just be rude.

The transcript that follows records two of the three Wriggle and Rhyme students answering the job interview question at the end of the course. The students were asked to simply tell about a research project they were involved in. Their answer is a typical representation of how students answered this question, although most transcripts recorded a single student's answer. The answers are chronological and provide an awareness of what they did, why they did it, how they overcame obstacles and what they would do differently next time. Betty and Angela told this story, finishing each other's sentences:

Betty: Initially we got put into groups and then we got given our project, but we were only given the context or title of our project, we weren't given any idea on what we were supposed to be researching, and then, so we had to go to Wriggle and Rhyme.

Angela: and meet our community liaisons, and set up a meeting, and meet them and find out what they wanted from us and expected from us and what we thought we could do.

B: And from there we kind of formed a topic surrounding developmental stages for the babies, and then we also had another topic, which was …

B: Initially [the community liaison] wanted us to study social isolation but we didn't feel that was strongly coming across, so we thought why force that if it's not really a key aspect. So our other little topic was key benefits for the mothers but then we kind of merged the two and decided we'd focus on benefits for mothers *and* babies. And from there we had to familiarise ourselves with the topic.

A: Then we had to do the lit review, find out the research and come up with a question.

B: Yeah it was after the lit review that we decided to merge the topics, because the lit review didn't really relate to anything we would be doing.

A: Yeah we had to do a lot of changes throughout the process, the more we got into the group, and the more we knew nothing was going to work, so we had to re-evaluate the situation. And then went from there and we had to decide on our methodology; like qualitative, quantitative, mixed. And we decided to do mixed.

B: Mixed is definitely most appropriate for us because like the mothers were really the source of information that we needed to use.

A: Because you can't really ask a baby questions.

B: So yeah we had to organise how we were going to go about doing that, and so that's when we got to know one of the mothers and then.

A: She told us it would be hard to do any individual interviews.

B: Yeah she said individual interviews would probably be a no go, so then we decided, well we talked to Martin, and decided that focus groups would be the best way to go with two groups of five.

A: And we had a meeting at the library to let them know where we were going, what was happening.

B: Yeah that we were going to hold those groups and stuff. And Martin also told us about Survey Monkey so yeah we set up the surveys.

A: So that we didn't break any ethical guidelines, we asked the librarian to send out the surveys from her database, so that we didn't have to get everyone's email address and we could be ethical.

B: Yeah and then we conducted the focus groups, after telling the mothers that we were going to be holding these groups in the next following weeks.

A: Between the focus groups we transcribed

B: and coded the information.

A: So it was all fresh in our mind at the time.

B: And when you do go through the interview again, you do pick up the themes, key ideas that you kind of forgot about in the interview.

A: And sort of doing the surveys, waiting for them, because we didn't send out the surveys until after we'd done the focus groups, so that got mothers coming to the focus groups, instead of just answering the surveys.

B: In hindsight we probably should have sent out surveys a bit earlier but we didn't really know that we were going to be doing that as well.

A: It was sort of last minute decision. Cos we did think of just handing out paper ones and getting them to fill them out there, but then most mothers up and leave straight after so that wouldn't work.

B: Yeah, they're tied up just feeding and getting the babies organised.

A: And now we're just at that analysing stage, going through step by step.

B: And we're going to put the report together!

There were variations on this job interview answer, but a concern that is remarkably absent in them is the description of fear. The learning from reading these transcripts was a lightbulb moment.

The students collectively were saying that their initial fear while meeting the liaison person and the participants was real but ephemeral. In the case of the three Wriggle and Rhyme students, as detailed elsewhere, their initial fear was being in the room where the music group took place. Their first task was to observe the group for 30 minutes. The students found the task overwhelming. The fact that this part of their story is absent above highlights their ability to look back and focus on the tasks and their achievements, not the fear.

The requirement for students to negotiate their research project with their designated organisation increased expectations for them and me. The price paid by me for this experiential learning was 24/7 availability. The students mentioned this in their transcripts and I confirm this. One factor made this possible. The small number of students was demanding, in response to my open-door office hours, but I was committed to this style of teaching. When students were asked about me, they invariably saw me as '"more like a mentor" than a lecturer:

Being able to contact Martin whenever you wanted was really helpful. Like I emailed him all the time I swear and he always replied like straight away. And he gave us his home phone number like in case you were in an emergency. It wasn't like a lecturer situation it was more like a mentor situation, which I liked more. It was different from a lecturer who just gives you things and says yeah just work it out yourself.

My availability in the mentor role was expandable, but not exhaustively. The optimum number of students is seven or eight groups of three students. The level of interaction with and among teams would not be possible were there 40 students in a classroom. This was similar to the optimum number of persons in a focus group: four participants is too small and ten too big.

Hauhart and Grahe (2015) recommend an awareness of staff:student ratios by limiting class size. Except for 2016, the capping of enrolment in the course has never been an issue. The numbers in each year have grown from 15 students to 30 students in 2016. In 2017, the number of students was an ideal 25. The 30 students in 2016 was five students—or two projects—too many. The ideal class size is 24, and if each group consisted of three students that would entail locating eight projects. The course meets twice a week, once for two hours and the other time for one hour. A great deal of time is spent in class having groups self-report on their progress. When more than 8 group reports are given in class, it is more difficult to retain the students' focus. In 2018, word-of-mouth endorsement of the capstone option in the humanities division will translate into the number of students enrolled in the course doubling in size to 50. To accommodate these numbers, I have made a timetable change, splitting the class in two, with 25 students in each class, meeting once a week for two sessions.

My teaching duties also involved attending interviews the students had with participants to provide on-the-spot coaching. My presence could extend an abbreviated four-minute phone interview into rich twenty-minute dialogues. The director of the *Gifted and Talented* programme wanted information on how the high school students experienced the course and what impact it had on their subsequent learning and social networks. She especially wanted to know what it was like being among students with similar abilities and returning to the regular classroom afterwards. Hilda from the Gifted and Talented group describes the impact of my intervention:

> I was so nervous for the first [interview], but we did it and we felt it went okay but then listening back on it, it was very short and like not very detailed like when we transcribed it there wasn't really any information there and we reckon that's because we were hand feeding them the answers and like I was doing all the talking and I don't know that carried on happening for the next three interviews but then for the next one [Martin] listened in and he told us like the big thing is to pause.

So we did that, and they went from like four minutes to like twenty-minute interviews, it was so good.

Four-minute interviews are not data-rich but they were experience-rich as they tended to be produced by a combination of close-ended questions, giving little time for the participant to answer. On my instructions, they rewrote the interview guide, focusing more on open-ended questions and moving away from yes and no answers. The second learning was how to use silence. Ask the question and then wait in silence. The third learning was getting the students calm.

I think Martin was a pretty calming influence especially when we hadn't had much progress in our report and he kind of said just calm down and guided us on how to do it pretty much.

As the students in 2013, and more so in 2014, stepped forward to assume more responsibility, I stepped back. As their confidence grew, I became more confident in them. I became more relaxed and further dismantled the scaffolding. I also spent even less time lecturing to the students in a move to a fully formalised tutorial or seminar setting where I expected the students each week to present more expansive collective descriptions of their projects in progress. This teaching method continued to be a successful technique for responding to issues or problems that individual groups had, which were likely shared by other groups.

Student-generated research sites

There were other significant changes to the scaffolding of the class. In years one and two, I had initiated and secured all the research sites. In year three, this restriction was relaxed. More groups of students were permitted to choose their own topics or research sites. This redirection occurred organically when, in week one of the course, I met with students individually to discuss their research interests and long-term goals, attempting to find the synergy between them and the six or seven projects I had secured. Unknowingly, this was a Hauhart and Grahe recommendation. They suggest creating enthusiasm by allowing students to select their own topics.

During these 30-minute discussions, two students independently mentioned that they were employed as support workers to physically and intellectually disabled children. They explained that they accompanied these children to a karate club for children with disabilities on Saturday mornings and they suggested that this would be a good site for research. Neither of them seemed keen on the projects I had found for them. With my encouragement, these students met with the lead karate instructor and he agreed for his organisation to participate in research. Unfortunately, the students were not keen to work with each other. One student made a video using footage filmed by a parent of one of the karate students. The other student made an advertising pamphlet. While the outcomes of these projects were successful, in subsequent years I saw a core learning outcome of the course being the students working in teams.

Having students working in teams was not always within my control. Late enrolments were a constant disruption. Early in the third year, an additional student wanted to join the class in the second week of the course, after all the groups had been formed. This was seen as having the potential to disrupt the developing micro work culture, or what Fine (1979; 1987) defined as an idioculture, of any group she joined. The student described her interest in the topic of sexual violence towards women, and her plans to research that topic in a subsequent postgraduate study. She contacted the local Rape Crisis centre and a project was initiated that the student could work on by herself. This illustrates the increased flexibility that was incorporated into the course in its third year. Subsequently, one group of two students studying student use of the central university library fell apart when a student left the university, leaving one student in a group of one. This student joined the Rape Crisis project that at that time had a single student working on it (see Chapter 9 for a full account of this study).

Student-generated research sites gave the students more autonomy but they also lessened my control over the feasibility and safety of these projects. At the time, I was writing the book *Planning Ethically Responsible Research* with Joan Sieber that included a chapter on the powerlessness and vulnerability of hired hand research (Seiber & Tolich, 2013, chapter 10). In many ways the students enrolled in Public Sociology were equally vulnerable. The chapter on hired hand research was subsequently listed as essential reading as it highlighted a number of proactive steps any researcher could take when he or she found him or herself in a risky situation. These steps were drawn from "A Code of Practice for the Safety of Social Researchers" (n.d.), and some of these are listed here.

- *Reliability of local public transportation.* Are reputable taxis companies easy to access? Is it safe to use private cars and leave them in the area?
- *Route planning.* Plan the route in advance, and always take a map. Study a map of the area for clues as to its character. Look for schools, post offices, railway stations and other hubs of activity. Think about escape routes from dense housing areas. Avoid going by foot if feeling vulnerable.

- *Assessing safety in buildings.* In multistory buildings, think about safety when choosing elevators or staircases.
- *Using alarm devices.* Carry a screech alarm or other device to attract attention in an emergency.
- *Contact information.* Let the interviewee know that you have a schedule and that others know where you are. Stratagems include arranging for a colleague or taxi to collect you, making phone calls or arranging for calls to be made to you. Leave your mobile phone switched on.
- *Alarm system.* Carrying mobile phones or personal alarms may be helpful as long as these are considered only a part of your comprehensive safety policy. Overreliance on mobile phones and alarms must not substitute for proper training in interpersonal skills.
- *Mad money.* Researchers should always carry enough money for both expected and unexpected expenses, including the use of taxis. It is sensible to avoid the appearance of carrying a lot of money, however, and to carry a phone card in case it is necessary to use a public telephone.

I gave additional advice to students' role-playing a situation if and when they felt sufficiently threatened in an interview with a participant to immediately leave the situation without seeking leave of the perceived threatening person. The instruction was to pull a cell phone from one's pocket as if it had vibrated and to answer the phone, speaking with some urgency to an imaginary family member and repeating the news that a relative was seriously ill and his or her presence was required. The student need only say, "that is tragic, I will be right there" and then leave the site, saying he or she will be in touch.

All groups were required to submit a safety plan that acknowledged the risks in their research site and how they planned to respond to these (see Appendix E).

The number of projects that I generated each year was always sufficient to sustain all student groups. However, I now follow Hauhart and Grahe's recommendation to create enthusiasm by allowing students to generate their own topics. This has other downsides. First, the creation of a topic and acceptance by the community liaison must happen within the first two-week period. Any longer and it breeds uncertainty in the students and disrupts the ongoing flow of the class.

The second downside of a student choice model is that it is often one student in a group of three who secures entry and these groups need monitoring so as to ensure that the other two students are given access to the securing student's project, thus mitigating any steps that could undermine teamwork.

Making students responsible for ensuring their own safety led to a great deal of independence, enhancing the students' experience of being a researcher and encouraging them to learn to cope with the frustrations that come with this role. It enabled students to be seen by their community liaisons and themselves as in the researcher role and to be accountable for the project. Development of this accountability was more important than the output that was actually produced. If the students finished the course knowing how and why they could do the research project differently next time, this would be an excellent outcome; they would have learned reflexivity.

Professional development: Micro steps

The internal mechanics of the four-part research project remained the same in 2013 and 2014 but the all-encompassing ethics application used in 2012 left the students anxious about meeting their responsibilities and they required some micromanaging. The causes of the fear varied between students, and it was difficult to predict what fear would emerge for which student. Some found it difficult to work in teams, some were shy and found it difficult to approach the organisation and some had difficulty with public speaking, which became evident when they were asked to make a collective report each week at the beginning of the class. One student's fear of public speaking was so severe that he was referred to either the university's student health centre or to Toastmasters. He chose the latter.

Teamwork was not straightforward as it produced unequal responsibilities. Students used an array of adjectives to describe their engagement with the project: nerve-racking, uncomfortable, petrifying, character building, humbling. Equally, some saw it as the most enjoyable class they had taken. Some students even found it difficult to be identified as a researcher representing the university. Some students were over-confident and evinced no fear. This occasionally led to problems developing rapport with either the community liaison or research participants. This incident came close to ending one project with a liaison person when a student interrupted them while they were working and asked a complex question about the organisation's mission statement. Not only was the question too complex, the timing was bothersome.

Students required assistance in other types of social engagement. For example, a requirement that all emails to liaison persons when convening the initial meetings be copied to me revealed lacklustre etiquette. It became apparent that the informality of these communications required attention and modification. Examples of professional development warranting modification were:

- Hey → I suggested Dear Anne
- You have not replied to my emails → I suggested students pick up the phone
- You have not replied to my emails!!!! → I pointed out the that the student's crisis is not the community liaison's

These digital communications were not predicted but easily resolved with common courtesy or by insisting on patience as a liaison took time to get back to the students. Delays also occurred when they recruited participants. At times, I had to step in and make some requests to participants myself. In the case of the gifted and talented group, my suggestion was to use the phone rather than email to recruit people. A student said:

> We hadn't received much interest from the students, and we couldn't start writing our report until we had interviewed the students, but we ended up getting over that by just emailing the organisers and asking if we could just ring them, so that was good.

No opportunity was lost in responding to the problems the students' research practice generated in the weekly class reports, and every mistake or frustration they had was translated into some form of professional development for them and for future students. For example, students were taught to slow down and respectfully create rapport with their liaison person or participants before beginning data collection. A good way to do this is to begin with some form of observation of the research site and build rapport. Rapport was defined for the students as at first introducing themselves to potential research participants and to talk about their interest in this particular community group. In other words, they were to present their intentions so that potential participants could make fully informed decisions about whether to participate. An additional rapport instruction involved suggesting that data collection begin with one person and analysing what he or she had to say before asking a second informant or respondent.

Delays in research, I explained, were inevitable, and "waiting" is an important skill for researchers to learn. Some teams of students met these challenges along the way but others spent considerable time in a state of frustration trying to establish a time when all of the team could meet their community liaison or waiting for research participants to sign up to take part in their project. In 2013, teamwork was essential for sharing the responsibilities.

> My project is a lot scarier; this is possible as it is something many of us have never done before. We rely on other people a lot more and

need to work with interpersonal skills … our obstacles are real, not hypothetical.

> The consequences are much greater if something goes wrong. You are letting more people down. And in this sense the task is a bit more challenging and scary.

Delays could also occur within teams. Group members reported frustration at finding that teammates did not have Wi-Fi in their flats or had insufficient funds to preload their phones. While time management is not a skill unique to research, it is a critical aspect of carrying out quality research. All students mentioned how their time management skills had improved due to the necessity of the project being completed within the 13-week semester and within a team. When asked what advice they would give to future students, most stated time management and organisational skills as being critical.

> We realised we didn't have much time so we set ourselves a deadline and got it done. Like we should have done that earlier as well. Setting ourselves deadlines helped, like we set ourselves a deadline not long ago and we were fantastic like we kept it in time.

Teamwork proved both stress relieving and stress generating for the students. Some students had never worked in teams before, and some found the expectation that they were to contribute to the team quite difficult. Nonetheless, students drew on each other's different experiences and were supported by this. For example, some students were terrified at the prospect of doing interviews, and others were not. For those who were fearful, observing someone else conducting an interview gave them the confidence that they could also conduct one.

Problems that developed when students conducted interviews should have led to a change of teaching practice. I did not realise it at the time, but the shortfall in students' confidence was not the student's fault, although it highlighted inadequacies in the ways students were prepared by the intermediate research methods course I taught that these students took prior to enrolling in the Public Sociology course. It was not until the development of the capstone course described in Chapter 7 that more attention was paid to integrating the previous year's research methods course and the Public Sociology Capstone. In short, it took a couple of years to comprehend what the students were explaining to me in their interviews about how the two courses were distinct, when I saw them as more integrated than the students did. For example, some students saw the intermediate research methods course as abstract—a typical Sociology course.

In the [intermediate research methods] I never had to fully think through the consequences of my actions because they were only theoretical. In Public Sociology I am constantly required to think through what is actually a practical method of doing things, and I have to take into account things like cost, time, and ethics—these aspects of study were limitless in the previous course because there was to be no practical application of the study. Overall, the Public Sociology course feels like a much more real-life, work experience type class, where I am learning the practical side of sociology, rather than the all theory based learning. Previously, I'd never conducted an interview, I'd never coded before, I'd never done anything so like hands-on, all I'd ever done is like readings texts oh this is how you do it, I'll just write that into my essay and just hand in my essay and out the information goes. But while you're actually doing it I feel like you retain it more. It's like, I like applying things to real-world situations, and that's something I definitely did in the paper which I really liked.

One student reflected on the intermediate research methods course and the Public Sociology course, describing the intermediate research methods course as preschool and Public Sociology as elementary school. Students did not, through this Public Sociology course, become competent researchers capable of independent research akin to a PhD or an academic. They did, however, become reflexive, and they came to view themselves not only as researchers but as responsible researchers working on projects even after the class had ended.

While there feels like there is less of a workload in the this [Public Sociology] class, it also feels more stressful because I am actually accountable to other people, including my organisation, my lecturer and my [study] partner—as well as the university itself.

Public Sociology mirrors "real life." We are tasked with meeting with an organisation, deciphering their needs and what we can do to benefit their organisation .... Actual research is carried out in the project rather than just theorised about and the final product that is produced will have real consequences for the relevant organisation it is produced for.

Students' journals characterised the Public Sociology course as being "real," in comparison with the more abstract research methods course. Public Sociology was an autonomous learning environment that pushed students to adapt to grasp hold of the entire research process. Reflective journals highlighted the fact that students were accountable to a community liaison and that they had internalised responsibility, not only to me, for the sake of a good grade, but also to the organisation. The journal entries differentiated between what I wanted and what the organisation needed, and showed an understanding that the organisation wanted something usable. The shorthand version of this is that organisations want to be evaluated: is their organisation relevant?

In 2013 and 2014, although their Public Sociology research loosely followed the same prescription as the intermediate research methods course, the students were correct to characterise the two courses as distinct. They found their Public Sociology projects as non-linear, cyclical and less structured, mirroring real life in the ways they were constrained by reality. Their projects were considered more realistic, involving learning on the job, as the projects linked ethical considerations with finite resources of time, money and a practical final output.

> The project has been a very humbling experience. I have come to realise that things I thought I knew or thought I could do and say, could in actuality put the validity of my research into question. The consequences of my actions are not just reflected on me, but could affect my [study] partner, my organisation, and perhaps even our research participants as well. I have always been highly self-motivated; but in this course my motivation is not for myself, but to be a good teammate and a useful source of research and information for the organisation. Taking this class has shown me how my research methods course can be useful in a real-world application, and that learning about research methods was and will continue to be an important aspect of my studies in sociology.

> The project is petrifying because you are responsible for your three people—I, the organisation, and your partner. Maybe there is a fourth master as you also want to make a difference with your project for the community.

The source of the accountability was the three or four "masters" that one student referred to (above): the lecturer, the organisation, the study partner and the wider community. Students were especially inspired by this relationship with the wider community. The students saw that they were connected to a Public Sociology, as they saw themselves having the potential to make a difference. Some students added a fifth master, the university, and noted, "While out in the field I am a representative of the university, and must be aware of the image I am projecting."

Although the students could call on me for advice, a lot more independence was demanded of the students. This was challenging, but also helped in the building of confidence.

> This sole responsibility encourages you to put all effort into the project to reach your full potential, because you feel that if you succeed in this paper you have the basic knowledge and confidence to complete projects in the future.

The Public Sociology course changed the students' perception of themselves in relation to their capacity to contribute to their community.

> The most important thing about our project is that I actually feel like I am making a difference, with the possibility of helping the community.

In 2014, there were lightbulb moments, if not a chandelier moment that helped generate the ethos of the course. The first was the change in the students' perception of their relationship with the organisation. They had a sense they were making a difference for a public good. This became reality in students' per- ceptions. This perception was thoroughly different from the more traditional inward-looking, self-obsessed internship model. By 2014, students reported that they had a sense of obligation to their organisations after only four weeks. In previous years this sense of responsibility had taken the full 12 weeks of the semester to emerge. This rapid socialisation into an accountability for the project was achieved because of the removal of much of the scaffolding that had initially been put in place to streamline the course—structures that, though well intentioned, took away essential learning opportunities for the students.

Sometime later, a serendipitous lightbulb moment came during my google search of US-based capstone courses. Online I found a letter that a now-retired California State University San Jose professor had sent his students. Professor Fallon's letter, reproduced here (with his permission), was sent to students enrolling in his forthcoming capstone course. The letter describes the capstone but also warns the students of the expectation for a high work ethic.

While I appreciate the sentiment of the letter, I have not had reason to replicate a similar letter. As said above, the work ethic he describes being necessary for successful completion of the capstone comes naturally to the students in my Public Sociology Capstone. Nonetheless, the letter is an excellent overview of the scope and expectations of a capstone course.

An Introductory Letter to my SOCI-181B Capstone Students

Dear Sociology Capstone Student, August 2013

Welcome! I have tried to create a most meaningful course for you. I love teaching this CAP, and I hope you'll value it too. A capstone intends to synthesize your four years of college/sociology education. It's a culmination of learning, and a last chance to "figure things out"! It is also a preparation and a transition into your future, a changing future at that. The course as I conceive it has four over-arching focuses: Self-Knowledge, Sociological Imagination, Community Engagement, Professional Development.

As I teach, this is not your traditional course, there are few lectures, but much interaction. I deem this course akin to an actual **job**, a professional assignment that demands a professional performance; and you'll be evaluated on that performance. In lieu of the 80-hour internship, the course incorporates a variety of campus & community experiences, and a minimum of 24+ hours of community engagement. A word of advice, strive to get off to a good start, because the workload increases significantly up to the end of your "work contract" which includes culminating **all four years** of your college experiences in a Learning PORTFOLIO.

Aware of your personal, social and WORK lives, this professor understands the demands upon your time; and respects your family commitments. I understand the high cost of education and your need to be employed. However, for this one last semester, this course needs to be a priority – over your social play, and yes, even over your work. Adjust your work to the demands of this course, it is a lesson in organization and time management! That said, today's work environment is a looser, freer, more fluid process than the '9–5', and accordingly I have structured the course much as "directed study." Still, class is critical to keep on track, to participate with peers, to apply thinking skills and assess values, and to evaluate your directed study learning.

Seeing your graduation in the context of our times, I have a degree of angst for you, and am compelled to guide you, given my experience and wisdom. For many, the "American Dream" is diminishing, and as if you don't know – life and career are NOT Business As Usual – but rather a "New Normal" that is reason for this capstone – to prepare you for a life after graduation as a Sociology major.

My concern teaching in the "Ivory Tower" is that curriculum may not match the contemporary reality you will encounter outside higher education. Therefore, this course will review your sociological studies to make "final sense" of your knowledge for "living in the material world", further your personal and professional development, assess the societal and global landscape for future opportunities, and engage you in community.

Lastly, a word about **my** teaching methodology and expectations for **your** participation and performance ... I integrate what are called High Impact Practices such as building a learning community, interfacing in collaborative learning groups, engaging community, etc. This course has a heavy workload, including a heavy **reading** load, and involves campus and community activities as well. Not all course readings and activities will be addressed in class, but demands self-responsibility, much as a job demands: know the syllabus, follow online communications, record activity and learning in an Activity Log & Journal! I believe in both quantity and quality of learning and your performance is evaluated accordingly. Note well this learning is not about a grade; but preparation for life! (Ask any student from my course what knowledge and skills they gained in one semester!) Trust the design of this capstone course by your Sociology professors, and maximize your effort and your learning. Strive to gain as much knowledge, skills, values and motivation as possible. Concentrate on mastering the course **objectives** always!

In exchange for all your work, I promise you a most valuable learning experience preparing and propelling you into a professional future in this ever-evolving, brave new economy. No more a "sage on the stage" but rather a "guide by the side" – I look forward to assisting you, butterfly, on your journey to become a professional in today's world, hoping to offer some sagacity and wisdom along the way, and fulfilling the Zen saying: **"Final job of teacher – free student of teacher!"**

Sincerely,
Michael Fallon, Professor

Note

1 This chapter draws on a journal article and a book chapter separately recording how the course was taught in 2013 and 2014. The first part of the chapter draws on Tolich, M., Scarth, B. & Shephard, K. (2015), Teaching Sociology students to become qualitative-researchers using an internship model of learner-support. *Journal of Social Science Education*, 14(4), 53–63. The second part of the chapter

draws on Tolich, M. (2015), Facilitating research mindedness in a Sociology research internship course. In K. van Heugten & A. Gibbs (Eds.), *Social Work for Sociologists: Theory and Practice* (pp. 157–170). New York, NY: Palgrave Macmillan. Permission has been granted from the journal and publisher and from the co-authors.

7 Getting it nearly right
Public Sociology Capstone 2017

In 2017, the sixth iteration of the course, the tumblers fell into place as Public Sociology fit within the capstone model. The course used the same four-part model (literature review, research design, data collection/analysis and final report) and had the students working in groups of three, drawing on their previous learning in research methods. Again, these tasks were augmented by the students' four reflective journals that had them review their experience of writing each part of their project. However, in 2017, the students' first reflective journal had a different format following along a suggestion by Hauhart and Grahe that was more aligned with their capstone model. I had them build their own personal learning and skills development portfolio (see Appendix C). The portfolio was similar to an annotated CV. The students listed the 20 courses they had taken at the university and gave a brief summary of the learning and skills development. The other three reflective journals were standard and had the students focus on their micro-interactions, such as meeting and greeting the liaison person as well as making contact with participants via the phone, email or cold calling. These reflections continued to throw up genuine moments of learning by doing in a non-linear, iterative style.

Twenty-five students enrolled in the Public Sociology course and worked on nine projects using an assortment of methodologies and final output mediums. Two projects employed a survey methodology:

- The organiser of *Poems in Waiting Rooms* wanted the students to evaluate this intervention by asking doctors' receptionists how the patients utilised the poems. They designed an online survey methodology but found that participants were more likely to complete the survey off-line using a hard copy version of the questionnaire.
- The *Riding for the Disabled* organisation wanted a study of how its other centres cared for their horses. For example, were the horses used for therapeutic purposes also rented out to able-bodied members of the

public? At the time, newspaper letters to the editor in the local newspaper had complained about the overuse of these horses when rented to the public.

Three projects employed a mixed methods design:

- Ninety-three *free libraries* had been established in Dunedin, each housing 20–30 books and sited outside a guardian's private home. The organiser wanted to know the experience of guardians' hosting the free library. The research began with seven interviews followed by a survey of the 93 guardians.
- *A blood donation* organisation wanted qualitative data describing the different reasons male and female blood donors did or did not donate blood. This initial qualitative data was used to create an online survey.
- *Quarantine Island* is an island in Dunedin Harbour. The group wanted a better understanding of the motivations of those visiting the remote island. This project began with a survey, fell into a focus group and ended by collecting life histories.

Three projects were based solely in qualitative interviews:

- The *Otago neighbourhood support group* had recently changed their name from the Otago neighbourhood watch and wanted to know how the police and other stakeholders viewed the group. Was the organisation relevant? The liaison person not only provided a list of the persons to interview, but also drove the students to these interviews.
- Alphabet Soup is a fledgeling *support group for LBGQT youth* in Dunedin who wanted the students to conduct interviews with other youth centres in other parts of the country to gain a better understanding of these groups' historical trajectory in terms of their strengths, weaknesses, opportunities and threats.
- A *foetal alcohol spectrum disorder* support group wanted the students to design a pamphlet for teachers describing the features of children with foetal alcohol spectrum disorder and then to interview teachers, asking them to appraise the utility of the pamphlet.

One project used interviews to create a video:

- The Blue Skin Bay Collective is *a climate change advocacy group* on the outskirts of Dunedin, and they wanted the students to create an informational video on the threat posed by climate change for coastal Dunedin.

Two projects, Riding for the Disabled and the foetal alcohol spectrum disorder support group, followed on as research sites from the previous year, but with new topics. It was interesting to me that the organisation Rape Crisis that had been researched so successfully for the three previous years was not chosen as a research site by the students.

It was also notable that two groups, the historical island site and the neighbourhood support group, were suggested and initiated by a class member in the course. As suggested in Chapter 6, these initiatives were both a blessing and somewhat problematic. In the first two weeks of the course, it was important for me to monitor these projects, making sure that the student who located the site allowed other students to participate in the planning of the research design. Having brokered entry to the site, this student was not writing a sole-authored project. This was most noticeable in one group during the weekly progress reports at the beginning of the semester. I had to intervene once during the initial class reports, requiring the person(s) who did not initiate contact with the community organisation to take a leadership role in making the verbal reports. Once this intervention was made, the project group members worked well together, sharing responsibilities.

The ethics process was again made even simpler in 2017. Students were required to write an ethics participant information sheet about their research topic for a non-present informant or respondent. They detailed what the research was about and what the participant would have to do. This was a straightforward exercise and was made easier by the ensemble of previous classes' information sheets that the students could utilise. They also had access to the TREAD (https://tread.tghn.org/) repository of ethics applications online.

Following Hauhart and Grahe's recommendation—*encourage ongoing learning by inviting past students to share their capstone journey*—past students of the Public Sociology Capstone were regularly tapped as a resource invited at the start of the course to share their journey through the four-stage process. They played their part using words like fear and frustration, which they eventually overcame for themselves and for their community organisation. Invariably, these descriptions present the course as the best class they have taken at university. If not the best, at least it was the most unusual, taking each of the students out of the comfort zone of the classroom and forcing them to confront how to present themselves as a social scientist. Plus, given that at least one three-minute video is made each year, these too are shown in class, allowing students to grasp the research process from data collection through selecting what soundbites to use in the final presentation.

Even though the course remained similar in content to the year two research methods course the students had taken the previous year, many students continued to report in their reflective journals[1] that they found the form of the Public Sociology course a formidable leap. They found the research methods course to be a theoretical course whereas the Public Sociology Capstone was about getting their hands dirty. A stumbling block of the capstone course was the enormity of the course's four parts:

> When I first began taking Public Sociology, I felt quite overwhelmed with both what to expect and what would be expected from me. I wondered how it was going to be possible to complete a research project and knew that I had a big hill to climb. Now that we are very nearly at completion with our study, I feel very confident in my ability to conduct a research project. I feel that the skills and experience I will take away with me are invaluable and will hold me in a strong position as I progress forward with my future studies and in my future employment opportunities. Prior to taking this paper, I felt I was a capable and confident speaker, able to meet new people and engage with them and a strong team player and I feel this paper has helped strengthen these skills.

As a lecturer, my learning in 2017 was the need to provide more hands-on learning for the Public Sociology course as these needs exposed weaknesses in the year two research methods course that I also taught. The previous course focused on how to create an interview guide or a questionnaire rather than how to conduct data collection. I now found that the Public Sociology students needed more role-plays on how to manage an interview or focus group. Thus, at various times in the semester, I responded to issues during the in-class reports.

On one occasion, a group of students were having trouble recruiting participants, more from inertia within the group than from resistance from participants. To jumpstart this group, I suggested that they begin to interview each other. The topic was attitudes to donating blood. When they later reported progress, I rewarded their initiative by suggesting they run a focus group in the class. Whereas in the previous second-year course students had written focus group questions, they had not themselves run a focus group. In preparation, I had the students watch a Richard Kruger YouTube video (Richard Krueger, n.d.) on running a focus group. (At the same time, I made time in my year two course I was teaching concurrently to show this instructive video also.)

The blood donation group then invited members of the class to take part in a focus group on their attitudes to blood donation. The outcome was a success on many fronts. One team member acted as moderator and one team member was the scribe. The moderator said:

> Running the focus group in class and having Martin there watching made me quite nervous but when the focus group ran smoothly and we

were praised for our efforts it was rewarding and gave me confidence in my own interviews and focus groups I had been running. Overall, the class has increased my confidence in a number of areas that could not have been gained in classroom lectures. The feeling of sense of achievement has been rewarding and my confidence over this course has definitely increased.

Other gaps in the students' learning were exposed. One group made a candid announcement during their weekly report which produced a genuine learning moment for the whole class. They described their first interview as a disaster. They reported they were so nervous they kept on saying "yes, yes, yes" as the person spoke, and if there was a pause, they asked the next question. My response to this—a situation I had seen before—may have shocked the class, but I told them how delighted I was that this had happened. I asked what can we could now learn from it. In other words, I wanted to reinforce in the student's minds that research is far from perfect. I told them that when they listen to an interview or read a transcript, there will always be times they could have asked a different question or should have asked a different question.

Later, one other student, who was present when this student revealed how disastrous that first interview had been, wrote in her reflective journal that her first interview with a participant was better for hearing this candid admission. She said that the disclosure made her more patient in the interview.

Candid revelations about false starts featured in the reflective journals:

> This paper allowed us to make mistakes and encouraged us to do so, so that we were able to learn from our experiences as we move forward which has been different from other papers taken. This paper has given me a new appreciation for research and I now know the commitment, time and passion needed to successfully complete a research project.

A second stumbling block students reported facing was similar to the previous year when they were faced with the realities of their project and how real its consequences were:

> By physically having to go out and met the group's organiser and put all the theory into practice was a big learning curve for me. I learnt how to conduct a formal meeting to find out the information and steps that they wanted to undergo in order to reach their goal for the project. Also I learnt how to set up and ethics report and all the background work that has to go into a research project before it can even start. The most

useful skill that I learnt was how to conduct a one on one interview with a participant, even though we had learnt this in the previous methods course last year, putting the skills into practice was very eye-opening. Knowing what questions to ask and keeping the discussion going and creating a comfortable environment for all parties evolved was essential to getting the best results.

The four-part structure of the course was not a stumbling block; in fact it was the opposite—the absence of a structure stumbled many students as they attempted to make many micro-decisions by themselves or within their group. Some micro-moments are obvious in hindsight but not so predictable in advance. For example, there is a distinct difference between giving advice on introductions and handshakes when meeting the liaison person for the first time, and the additional advice to make these introductions quick and assertive.

A group member recorded in her reflective journal how her group's tardy introductions were problematic; they failed to introduce themselves at the first meeting and they were concerned, if not frustrated, on how to alleviate the situation by awkwardly reintroducing themselves at the second meeting. The three female students never progressed being referred to as "the girls."

In previous years, as outlined in Chapter 5, students were encouraged to write more formally. "Hi" or "Hey" were not appropriate email salutations. In 2017, I noticed in the first two weeks that students continued to write emails to me using very informal language. In response, students were encouraged to use the term "Kia Ora" (Hello in Maori and used in many academic email communications) in all email communication and how to greet their community liaison on the first visit. In the main, they obliged. This was a step up from an email salutation as "Hey."

In 2014, when students began to choose their own research sites, I responded by instigating a safety plan for each group. For example, I had discussed the students' apparel in terms of safety. In 2017, I gave more instructions on the type of clothes they should wear for their first meeting. The basic instruction was to dress as if they were going for a job interview. Yet one student's reflective journal reported that he remained so sartorially muddled, he failed to make notes on the meeting. Obviously, I had overlooked the division of labour within a team that should have designated one note taker:

> My mind was still riddled with questions about the first meeting; how we were supposed to dress, what we were supposed to ask her, what were we meant to find out, and did we need to take notes during the meeting? Martin helped us with telling us how to dress, and one of his

guest speakers told us that they made the mistake in their first meeting of writing too much down and not overly engaging in the conversation. However this led to none of us taking notes and I now know that it would have been best to plan our questions, have one person ask and one person take notes. The answers I now have for the above questions have raised my confidence and can only be attributed to the experience I had and the failures me and my group made.

The course would not be possible without the students' willingness to work as a team, pooling knowledge and effort and showing resilience when things did not go well, especially when participants were difficult to recruit. From the reflective journals in 2017 and also from one-on-one meetings in office hours, students revealed their past and current experiences with the micro-politics of producing a joint research outcome dependent upon others. The list of micro-politics issues expanded around demands of working with a team outside the bounds of a structured classroom.

Because this project involved a lot of outside of class work as well as a number of different tasks, there was the need to ensure that we were able to allocate tasks and organise meetings with the liaison and participants that could suit all three of our schedules. Therefore my confidence in working within a team for a practical and multidimensional project such as this one was effectively increased.

Teamwork was not an unknown to these students—some entered the course with baggage. A reflection shared that previous teamwork in other classes had been problematic:

I have done a few group projects before but none to the extent of this research project, which made the prospect of working through Public Sociology with someone I did not previously know quite daunting. However, from the start my partner and I reassured each other we were both committed and balanced responsibilities – contacting people, booking study rooms, and completing assignments – out equally between us, making sure to always keep each other in the loop. Recently we discussed how the responsibility we felt to each other actually motivated us both to be more organised than we would be for individual projects! Overall the success of working with my team member has strongly bolstered my confidence in the idea of working with other people in the future.

Teamwork will always be an unknown variable as part of this non-classroom-based structure. In the past, I have intervened in these group disputes, but more recently I have met with the factions and encouraged them to find a way to negotiate a way forward. One serious dispute in 2017 occurred in and around the production of the final report. One student had track-changed the final report whereas the other members were writing the report. Wisdom of Solomon suggested that there was some serious learning to be had at this late stage of the project. Rather than demanding that all parties contributed to the final report, I had them take a big step forward and discuss among themselves how they would collectively create and present the final verbal report.

What happened here was a type of flexibility needed in teaching a Public Sociology Capstone. By then, the four reflective journals were finished but I would have liked to have those students explain how it was that they were so successful in putting their differences behind them and negotiating the final act of the course in their seamless public presentation. As a teacher, this renegotiation and successful presentation was a cherished teaching moment. The students' dispute was entrenched and likely to be similar to many moments they will encounter in the workforce when negotiating conflict. Moreover, resolution of conflict is a common interview question and these students would be greatly advantaged by resolving this moment of conflict as well as they did.

There will always be variability of skills and effort by the students and this was masked to some effect by the teamwork. In 2017, I discovered that the nine groups were variable too. A random variable was the liaison's degree of involvement in the students' project. It was well known that initial meetings were always a daunting task, but the liaison's level of commitment to their projects was uneven and for many it was a motivator to produce a good project. Some felt the motivation as pressure:

> Working with a community group was a totally new experience for me, but something I have now also gained a lot of confidence in. I had no idea what to expect when I turned up on her doorstep one drizzly March afternoon, but quickly realised that she put a lot of time and effort into her cause which really motivated me to want to do a good job of research for her. I knew I would feel terrible if we let her down which once again was a huge motivator to be organised and on-top of the project at all times, which I liked.

In 2017, two projects, the Free Library Project and the Poems in Waiting Rooms, had the same community liaison. She was more of a facilitator than a person who empowered. She gave the free library group the residential addresses of potential participants and their email addresses. For the Poems in Waiting Rooms, she provided the addresses of the doctors' waiting rooms where the poems had been left. Beyond this, the students had to navigate their way to the places that housed the free libraries or to the doctors' waiting rooms and cold call the receptionists. But there was great variability in gaining access.

Contacting the persons (guardians) of the free library was straightforward, and the students could contact these people by knocking on their doors in the late afternoon or during the weekend. Access to the doctor's waiting rooms caused logistical problems. How could they be introduced to the receptionists during normal working hours? This group's persistence paid off as invariably they were forced to meet the receptionist on one visit and return to receive the completed hard-copy survey on the second visit. The reward here comes from this persistence rather than the response rate and was graded in a similar way to a diving competition; each project had its own degree of difficulty. A member of the poems group reflected the difficulty back to me, which I read as tenacity:

> Reaching out to survey participants was the aspect of our project I found the most difficult. I am a little sensitive and anxious by nature and – knowing the stigma surrounding "annoying surveys" – the thought of turning up at numerous waiting rooms around Dunedin pushing for people to complete our survey was slightly terrifying! The receptionist at our first survey was quite sour which decreased my confidence even more, so my teammate and I decided to do the next few surveys together which improved both our levels of confidence enough that we decided split the rest to deliver solo. I can now honestly say I no longer find this difficult and feel reasonably confident in approaching members of the public to do surveys – a valuable research skill!

Much of this book has highlighted the systematic dismantling of the scaffolding from this course. However, there was more scaffolding added—at least that was the intention. One disappointment in 2016 was planning for but being unable to fulfil a goal I had set for the students. I had intended for the students to celebrate their projects with a public presentation in front of their fellow students and the community organisations. This, I was later to learn, was one of Hauhart and Grahe's recommendations— *invite students to make a public presentation of their research project.* Unfortunately, due to illness, I was forced to cancel this presentation. The students then went on to make in-person presentations. In 2017, this final project was presented to the liaison persons and invited members of faculty. As part of this presentation, each student was given the opportunity to provide a simple statement of how this Public Sociology course enhanced his or her undergraduate degree.

In 2017, there was still a need to add some scaffolding to fulfil the capstone prescription that the students' final report be publically presented. Although the students practised their verbal presentations in class prior to the public presentation, the expectation that the students make a five-minute presentation to strangers was a daunting task. The tendency for these students was to go through their report chronologically, taking far too much time with the literature review and leaving little time for the presentation of results.

To alleviate this tension, I gave the students a possible structure for their talk. I wrote on the blackboard the instructions (see Appendix D) for their verbal presentation, which the students duly followed in their written report.

The verbal presentations were well done, and each was accompanied by PowerPoint slides. I was very proud of the students for the relish they took in getting up there and presenting their findings.

In addition, I chose two confident students to serve as Master of Ceremonies. I had been prepared to fulfil this role and I was surprised that both of them said they would love to do it. They did a remarkable job, making sure that each PowerPoint slides was up and ready for the next speaker who they introduced using all of their first and second names. They also ad-libbed a script I had written for them explaining to those present, especially faculty interested in the capstone aspect of the course, how the course fitted into a capstone model.

As previously mentioned above, I asked the students to use their first reflective journal to create an inventory of the classes they had taken as an undergraduate and (using an economy of words) documenting the learning and skills they gained in each class. My plan at the end of the course was to ask these students to annotate their inventory, noting what skills they had drawn on in the Public Sociology course as well as what new skills they developed in the Public Sociology course itself. This revision could have been done more systematically as students tended to write reflections rather than revising their previous skills and learning portfolio. Regardless, the outcome was the same as what follows, providing a number of students' descriptions of how the course enhanced their prior learning.

The first description needed two statements to capture the capstone effect. The student's first final reflection stated:

> This paper gave me immense satisfaction as I could clearly see that everything I had learnt in previous years was effectively applied in a practical context. Public Sociology taught me far more than what I could have learnt in any classroom. It was exponentially rewarding to see that what I have learnt in the past three years has not gone to *waste*.
>
> (my emphasis)

To me, it was very unusual for me to follow up on a student's reflection, but I did ask the student about the word "waste" and she elaborated:

> So in essence I was trying to show how excited I was that all the information I had learnt in the past three years, such as theories, was not wasted or forgotten. This was demonstrated when information I had learnt was practically applied in this paper. Throughout the semester, things such as the labelling theory and theories behind qualitative interviewing popped up most days. This was rewarding to know that all those days I spent studying and listening to sociologists and other lecturers talk were not one-offs, and that the information would continually be a part of my life especially during this year, and in the years to come where I may potentially delve into more research.

A second student captured the incremental nature of this learning:

> One of the skills I have gained throughout this [Public Sociology] course is the ability to conduct a one-on-one interview in a confident and professional manner. Prior to this course I had never conducted an interview and therefore I see this as one of the most valuable skills I have gained. In the previous course that I completed in the previous year, qualitative methodology was explored and we were taught how to properly conduct a qualitative interview and formulate an interview guide. However, for me, *this was only ever words on a lecture slide or on the pages of a textbook.* The current course has given me the ability to turn these written words into practice, which I found was a lot more difficult than anticipated. On review of the first interview I conducted with the participants I was very nervous, often stuttering and engaging too frequently in a conversational manner rather than listening to what the participant had to say and giving them time to fully answer the question or elaborate. However, by the fourth and final interview that I conducted, after revision of the original questions and self-critiquing, I was evidently more confident in the questions I was asking which was reflected in the clarity of my words. By this final interview I was also more confident in my ability to listen to what the participant was saying and using this to prompt and ask up follow up questions in relation to the contextual references they were providing.
>
> (My emphasis, developed in Chapter 11)

A third reflective journal entry was also comparative:

> The Public Sociology course is different to the courses I have previously completed within sociology as it goes beyond theory and allows

students to apply our skills and knowledge to a tangible, real-world project. It is also different to the research I have completed for physical geography courses in two significant ways. The first is the ethics component; generally it is not necessary to ask physical processes for their consent before examining them. The other is the necessity of interacting with people outside of the university. In the Public Sociology course we not only interview members of the public, we also report to them, which I have never had to do in any other paper.

The Public Sociology course allowed this student to link her skill attainment in all her classes together:

> I have also learnt to trust that I have to skills and motivation to do these things. I have actually attained skills I didn't even realise I had through previous papers – these skills, such as being able to write concisely, communicate findings effectively, analyse information and work in a team, have all allowed me to be successful in this paper. This paper has also allowed me to develop these skills further.

My reflection on this 2017 course was how much more the community groups were integrated into the class. Students met them regularly and at the end of the course, they showed the students genuine appreciation for their efforts. A second reflection was that I could have done more with the learning and skills portfolio. It should not have been a reflection but a single assignment worth a percentage of the grade. In 2018, I expect to integrate this learning and skills portfolio as a means to an end by having students add to it and revise it in each of the four reflection exercises. Having said that, students in 2017 can augment their CVs with a formal academic transcript fleshed out by a concise description of the skills and learning developed over three years. Perhaps their parents might grasp what it was they did at university during the three years.

Note

1 Ethics approval was sought from the University of Otago to contact all of the students in the 2017 course after the exam grades were finalised, asking them for permission to confidentially quote excerpts from the reflective journals. Ten students contacted me directly or via an intermediary and gave approval.

8   Messy, creative coaching

Teachers who follow this capstone research-based model need to be aware of a personal caveat. I offer a note of caution for those seeking promotion based on student evaluations. In 2017, I sought a double merit increase and was only successful in a single merit increase based on my publications rather than my less-than-stellar student evaluations. The Public Sociology Capstone will never rank highly in terms of organisation. The beginning of the semester has the students working in teams with unfamiliar people, meeting their community liaison for the first time and coming to grips with the research design of the project. This initial period is frenetic and difficult to organise. The students dutifully and literally answered the question on the university's student evaluation questionnaire.

Comment on Martin Tolich's organisation of the course.
The rank score was low.

The students were also asked a second question:

Did Martin Tolich's teaching stimulate your learning?
I did score highly on the second question. One reflective journal recorded:

> Public Sociology included many new experiences for me. I had never carried out a research project in full before. The new experiences included having to approach a community group and send professional emails. Work full time in a group project, present our literature review to the organisation, apply for ethics consent for our research, devise a safety plan, run a test survey, recruit respondents through phone calls and in person – this required some form of scripting. New experiences also having to code our own data, and then further analyse and provide outcomes and recommendations. These new experiences have

enhanced my confidence in group work, my professional mannerisms and all of these other new experiences.

There is a messy explanation that justifies the low organisational score the students gave me. In the past year, these discouraging scores on organisation were offset by reading Tim Harford's book *Messy: How to be Creative and Resilient in a Tidy-Minded World*. His book only encourages learning via messiness found in the organised chaos of a Public Sociology Capstone.

In late 2016, I found great comfort in learning of Tim Harford's *Messy* book. It epitomises the pedagogy of this Public Sociology Capstone, as the course at times could easily be labelled organised chaos or chaos organised. Harford provides an example of organised chaos in traffic rules in European villages. Some of these towns, he says, erase all street signs and replace the black tarmac with cobblestones. He writes:

> *a confusing situation always grabs the attention* .... Perplexed, drivers took the cautious way forward: they drove so slowly through the town that the researcher could not normally capture their speed on the radar gun. This logic forced drivers to confront the possibility of small errors, the chance of them making the larger ones was greatly reduced.

Messiness is the Public Sociology Capstone's pedagogy. This instruction is simple and is worth reiterating. Students working in groups of three with a basic background in research methods are sent off to meet a community organisation and they are then required to construct a research design and implement it. This *confusing situation grabs their attention* and they do make small errors, knowing that their lecturer is less a teacher and more a coach. This learning is different from an internship, where students absorb experience in situ as if by osmosis. In the capstone, the students' task is guided by prior learning and they validate this learning process.

> Public Sociology has been the most unique paper I have taken while being at University. The learning curve in this paper has been huge in comparison to my experience of other papers. The theoretical side of research had prepared me for many aspects of carrying out a research project, however there were so many new things I learnt that you could not learn through theory.

Messiness was integral to the Public Sociology Capstone in 2017, but it was also a fundamental tenet of the course at the outset in 2012. For example, in 2012 and in subsequent years, I embargoed the exam questions because each year I wanted to ask the same question that exposed the disorderliness of Public Sociology by asking the students "how they would do this project differently." In other words, I was less interested in what they did and more interested in how they would do it differently next time—what they had learnt. A reflective journal entry early in 2017 stated:

> My group and I struggled with the literature review and the research design especially, yet now I would approach both of these things very differently. I would plan the literature review before beginning the researching and understand the limitations required to work in before deciding the method. I think the largest difference between the intermediate research methods course and the Public Sociology Capstone is doing the research instead of only planning it.

Upon reflection, my experience teaching this course was always subconsciously developing a useful user-friendly course rather than scoring higher evaluations, and within the messiness a new form of teaching developed organically that I now recognise as a capstone. The course is both student intensive and teacher intensive.

In some early journal articles I wrote about this course, I was loose in how I defined core concepts such as internships, and usually I casually called myself a coach rather than a teacher. I said this without conceptualising what an internship or a coach's role was. Intuitively I thought of the coach I wanted to be as a person who sat in a classroom and allowed my students to share their mistakes and successes in their verbal reports each week, updating each other on their progress. I was there to answer questions, but I was also there to seize opportunities to explain nuance or suggest different ways of conducting research. This messy learning by doing philosophy that guides this course allows students to make mistakes and learn from these mistakes. I too have made mistakes, most notably how I interacted with the community liaisons in the first year of the course. I misread their willingness to be fully involved in the students' work.

In July 2017, after completing the sixth iteration of the Public Sociology Capstone, I had an opportunity to take part in a half-day professional development seminar offered at the University of Otago that featured coaching for managers. The course had a take-home message that both reinforced how I was coaching my students but also how I was refining that process.

I learned that a coach was a person who does not give advice but rather creates a process for students (or individuals) that allows them to define and resolve their problems. One useful anagram was the GROW template ("The GROW Model," n.d.).

What is the person's goal?
What is the reality of this being achieved?
What are the options?
What is the way forward?

In retrospect, I can see myself systematically attempting to become a coach as the Public Sociology Capstone course developed. Intuitively, I was removing more and more of the scaffolding that held the course together. For example, the ethics application I wrote for my students in year one produced too much scaffolding. Over the years, I provided less and less scaffolding for my students and allowed them to make mistakes and rectify them. The GROW model is a further step towards taking scaffolding away in 2018.

The developing coaching role only presents itself now because I have the confidence in myself and in my students. The coaching role legitimates the taking away of as much scaffolding as possible. In future iterations of the course, I will do less and less for the students and I will have them establish the goals and decide if the goal or goals are plausible in reality, and have them come up with options to deal with a messy reality and find a way forward for themselves. I know they can do it.

In terms of coaching, I could ask myself the same exam question I asked my Public Sociology students: Don't tell me what you did, but how would you do it differently? The most significant innovation in future capstones will be implementing the GROW coaching model. My **goal** is to continue to provide less and less scaffolding for my students. I want them to spend more time reflecting on the skills and learning, specifically from the second-year course but also from all of their courses they had taken previously. The **reality** of this is to continue to allow them to make mistakes, but I also need to teach them better in the second-year research methods course. The **options** are the students; what are the advantages and disadvantages of trying one strategy over another? The **way forward**, making sure that the students' goals are not large, was solely focused on four parts of the research project but recognised the micro steps that are involved in the successful completion of this course.

In the six years, some of my core assumptions changed. Chapter 5 reported how my interviews with community liaisons were prompted by a fear of the sustainability of my courses. Could it continue to secure community support in a small city? Writing in 2017, now from the perspective of hindsight, I question this core assumption. To my surprise, in the past six years the ability to generate research sites for my students has never been a problem. Sustainability is important but is not life or death.

Most years I kept a file of possible research sites for the next year. For example, on a morning exercise walk I noticed one of 93 "Lilliput Libraries," letterbox-size free libraries in Dunedin. Once sited, the topic went into a file. Sites are everywhere and the community groups are eager to have a connection to the university. I say this to encourage those wanting to adopt a Public Sociology model that people in the community are eager to be part of the university. Equally, and this is a *major* learning on my part, is that one of the true benefits of the Public Sociology course is that it allows me to interact with my community. In many ways, the course I teach is my Public Sociology and each year I get to learn more and more about the people of Dunedin. Having said that, a great deal was learned from exploring the sustainability of the course in 2012. I pick up there and recount the community liaisons' opinions about sustainability and what they got, or did not get, from being involved with the students.

There will be other changes going forward in 2018. Even before I completed grading the final examinations in 2017, a number of changes for future iterations became apparent. First, responding to the Driving Miss Daisy (elder taxi service) liaison person (mentioned in Appendix F)—she suggested that students in 2018 should be able to continue research previously conducted by students in the Public Sociology course. This action produces a longitudinal aspect to the research and returns to the sustainability of community collaboration I sought in Chapter 5. Maybe the course in 2012 was not stable enough to warrant seeking sustainability, but it is now. This innovation has spinoffs. It is likely to tie the current 2017 students as mentors to the students enrolled in the 2018 course. This would further cement one of Hauhart and Grahe's core prescriptions for a capstone.

One major scaffolding change will develop in the Public Sociology Capstone in its relationship to the year two research methods course that precedes it. For example, the structure I presented to the Public Sociology students as a possible outline for their verbal presentation exposed a weakness in both the Public Sociology course and in the second-year research methods course. Thus, I will ensure the learning goes two ways. I need to spend more time in the second-year research methods course giving examples of how to run focus groups and one-on-one interviews and how to code data thematically. In general, quantitative survey questions are well catered for. The Public Sociology course will continue to provide additional scaffolding to assist students to condense their 3000-word written report into a concise five-minute verbal report.

There is room for other changes—maybe an academic memoir on Public Sociology Capstones. The parents I met at graduation in 2008 challenged me, if not threatened me—spurring me to seek out pathways for their children that enhanced their sociological learning beyond vague marketed destinations. In many ways, I believe this response is one of the major accomplishments of my academic career. At no time did I see this book emerging nor did I set out to write a book or this reflective autoethnographic account. The outcome was organic. The pathway I followed was intuitive, based on 20 years of teaching rather than informed by any learning and teaching pedagogy. For example, I was aware of internships but I was not acquainted with the concept of a capstone. I went on to construct the Public Sociology Capstone, for a few years loosely following an internship model, but I never formally defined an internship other than seeing it as learning outside the classroom. Additionally, at the time I did not realise that there were a number of internship models and that the one that I was following was not a traditional model. Traditional internships had students domiciled within an organisation, producing self-centred outcomes. My Public Sociology Capstone version of an internship was fundamentally different.

The distinction between a domiciled internship and a library-based research internship was intuitive. My goal was to highlight one pathway towards a government or non-government agency policy analyst position (or lifelong social activism) rather than any generic job. My sense was that students could make those vague connections between their degree and a generic job all by themselves. My role was to demonstrate that there was a pathway to a specific set of occupations that drew on their sociological knowledge and skills.

When the course began in 2012, I was unaware of the capstone model, but the course was linked to the Public Sociology model and—looking back now—the capstone expectations as outlined by Hauhart and Grahe (2015) are scattered throughout the book. While not following this prescription, they were always subconsciously there. The Public Sociology model gave the students the opportunity to use their prior university learning in the Public Sociology course. At first, this prior learning was limited to the intermediate research methods course I taught but in later years students were required to marshal all of their prior learning to fulfil the requirements of the capstone. Their annotated CV (see Appendix C) was drafted in the first Public Sociology Capstone course in 2017, recording skills they gained in all their university education.

If you define something as real it is real in its consequences. How I have defined differences between internships and capstones is not just analogous; they are different. Capstones are neither neoliberal nor an internship. And here, again, with the benefit of hindsight, I can make a distinction between the ethos that Burawoy challenges us with his Public Sociology and internships universities market as "work integration" or "work ready." Public Sociology by its very nature focuses on other people's problems. Neoliberalism tends to focus the students inwards, on themselves.

9 Like sherbet dropped in lemonade

Student stories

This chapter is a celebration of the outputs of three separate studies conducted in years three, four and five of the course. The first output is presented in Appendix F in the form that it appears on a blog on the senior citizen taxi service company's website. It resulted from the students' ride-along observations of a senior citizen taxi service. The two studies reported below are combined and reflective, written by two students from different years who previously did not know each other. They were both involved in a study on behalf of the organisation Rape Crisis. In 2014, students analysed existing survey data for Rape Crisis and the second year—2015—other students conducted unstructured interviews with stakeholder organisations that referred persons to Rape Crisis. The intrigue with these two Rape Crisis studies is how absorbed the students were in both working for Rape Crisis as an organisation and the mortification that their findings could, if true, potentially harm the organisation.

The text is written as a collaborative writing exercise by two former Public Sociology students, Kayla Stewart and Morgan Speight,[1] that I instigated once it became apparent that students using a different research technique in different years had a Public Sociology experience that changed their lives. The conclusions they reached made them see themselves as legitimate social scientists willing and able to make a contribution.

Kayla and Morgan met because I saw a parallel in their projects and I suggested they write a dual-authored article (Stewart & Speight, 2016) comparing their Public Sociology experiences from different years. What happens when a student finds fault with their organisation's practice? As they sat in my office, I placed an audio recorder between them as asked each to provide an account of their research experience with the organisation Rape Crisis to each other. As expected, a "snap" moment took place, as each saw themselves in the other's experience. What resulted was methodologically a shared ethnography (a duoethnography), what Norris, Sawyer and Lund (2012) describe as a collaborative methodology in which two or more researchers juxtapose their life histories in order to provide multiple understandings of a social phenomenon to create dialogic narratives from multiple perspectives. The dialectic process of creating a duoethnography is also designed to be transformative to the writers.

Although both students took the Public Sociology course in different years, when they first met over an audio recorder, they and their stories were eerily similar. They were both fifth-year law students and Sociology majors at the time they undertook the Public Sociology course. Since that time, they have talked endlessly about the life-changing events. Yet sitting at my office table with the audio recorder switched on was their first taste of writing for publication.

Kayla Stewart enrolled in the Public Sociology course wanting to augment her Law Honours thesis that included an analysis of sexual violence legislation and she asked Rape Crisis Dunedin (hereafter Rape Crisis) if they would assist her with her Public Sociology project. At this point, although Kayla had chosen a research location, she had not yet developed a "topic."

In 2015, Morgan Speight and two other women in the Public Sociology class went through the door Kayla had opened and they too sought a topic for their research project from Rape Crisis Dunedin. The article that follows is told in narrative form, letting Kayla and then Morgan tell their stories as they told it to the other. Kayla begins by documenting the 2014 study.

The 2014 study—Kayla Stewart

Rape Crisis is an organisation that I really value and I hoped that I would be able to collaborate with them on a project that would benefit the organisation as well as providing a unique learning opportunity for me. I made contact with the organisation and met with the members as a group. This is because Rape Crisis operates from a collective principle rooted in feminist ideology whereby decisions are made across the board rather than via a top-down hierarchical process. Consequently, all women of the collective were informed about what I might be doing and how the research would operate. As part of their work, Rape Crisis provides education to high school students in the Otago region in the form of rape prevention education workshops. Following these workshops, students fill in a customer satisfaction survey. At the time Rape Crisis had nearly 750 surveys, all un-coded.

In my second week, a student's Public Sociology project fell through and subsequently another law student and Sociology major, was approved by Rape Crisis to join the team tasked with collating the data. Our first step was to enter the raw data onto a spreadsheet and collate the results looking for strengths and weaknesses of the program. At first the methodology was simple—comparing apples with apples and examining how the Rape Crisis high school workshops performed across the various outcome measures. We then isolated a year level, year eleven (aged 15), in the same calendar year from two different schools but different deciles; one was decile five (mid-range SES) and the other was decile ten (highest SES). These students received the same workshop presentation but when we compared the results from these schools, the overall satisfaction levels were different. The students from the decile ten schools rated the workshop more effective on every single outcome measure. This was an epiphany moment, as we were not expecting to find anything of significance.

Whilst exciting for us, we knew this kind of analysis would be useful to Rape Crisis who strive to present quality programs that are beneficial to all recipients. The question then arose as to what this difference could be attributed to: whether the problem could be sourced to the survey instrument itself, which could be consequently adjusted, or if the efficacy of the program differed for students drawn from different socioeconomic areas or something else entirely.

In our quest to explain this unexpected finding, we did two things. First, we critiqued the survey and made concrete recommendations to address and control for the imbalance. We revised the Rape Crisis survey instrument because in our report we claimed it was inadequate for the evaluative task. Some survey questions were vague and ambiguous. For example, the question "Did you learn anything?" which is a yes/no question provided four responses to choose from and two of these were essentially the same: 'nothing new' and 'I didn't learn a thing.' It also became apparent that the way in which one particular question was asked might have resulted in confusion amongst students. For example, the question 'what did you think of the workshop-likes/dislikes?' The students often interpreted this as a closed question asking whether they liked or disliked the workshop, circling their answer as opposed to providing an unstructured response.

The restructuring of the survey suggested more objective questions that did not require a praise-based response.

- 'What percentage of sexual assaults involve alcohol?'
- 'What is the most commonly used 'date rape' drug?'
- If someone tells you they have been sexually abused, how should you respond to them?'

This new objective standard measured the course content (including rape myths and attitudinal change) by evaluating what was learnt.

The second task involving the socioeconomic discrepancy was more complicated. We returned to our original literature review and focussed on an article written by Briggs and Hawkins (1994) that evaluated the effectiveness of the 'Keeping Ourselves Safe' program. It was a personal safety curriculum implemented in New Zealand schools. In that study, children from lower socioeconomic groups had a different response to the program based on significantly lower knowledge and skill levels than their middle-class counterparts and children from the middle-class group gained more from the program. Thus socioeconomic status was shown to be a factor influencing the effectiveness of these types of programs.

Briggs and Hawkins (1994) only partially explained our results and we sought further explanations in a class analysis of children's behaviour. Hochschild's Managed Heart (1983) discussed the commodification of human emotion and drew on Bernstein's (1975) analysis that this display was class-based. British middle-class and working-class families made distinctions between two types of family control—positional and the personal. The positional have clear and formal rules—"do as you're told" whereas the personal control is "it would really make me happy if you would do that for me now" so is actually more emotional. In personal control, children are taught (inter alia) that their feelings are important and the evocation of these feelings is encouraged. We hypothesised then that those from higher socioeconomic backgrounds i.e. decile ten, were more inclined to give praise than those from higher socioeconomic backgrounds in light of them more willing to express their emotions. Thus an explanation in the divergence in the students' results pointed to a classed based analysis. Yet this conjecture as we described below in the duoethnography is only half the story; we had to tell Rape Crisis the grim news that the data they had collected was potentially confounded by class.

The 2015 study—Morgan Speight

When my group and I approached Rape Crisis, we were given a different task, one that involved the referral process to Rape Crisis that is at the heart of Rape Crisis practice as women who have been subjected to sexual violence can be referred to Rape Crisis for assistance. The problem Rape Crisis faced was they had been receiving data from referrals in terms of whether certain organisations had been or had not been referring to them when presented with a case of sexual violence. These organisations were first responders, the police and DSAC (doctors for sexual abuse care). Rape Crisis had noticed that the numbers of referrals from these organisations were not balanced. The police were very effective at referring women to Rape Crisis but DSAC were less forthcoming. Often DSAC would refer a woman to Victim Support who would then act as a middle person and refer the woman to Rape Crisis. Whilst Victim Support could refer to Rape Crisis, this was not the most efficient method. Our project quickly became an investigation into this discrepancy. Rape Crisis wanted to know why DSAC were not referring to them.

The research design was straightforward. We planned to conduct interviews with the police, DSAC and Victim Support in order to understand if DSAC were reluctant to refer to Rape Crisis. The research team conducted interviews. Rape Crisis had informed us that unlike DSAC, the police way of thinking was progressive and fluid, constantly being adapted to align with recommendations put forward by Rape Crisis and other organisations alike.

Rape Crisis' hunch that there was something amiss in the way DSAC referred people was correct but upon further analysis this finding flawed us. In the two interviews, DSAC literally put a different label (Becker, 1974; Lemert, 1981) on "rape." DSAC said that women who reported to them were less likely to think of what had happened to them, as rape and DSAC did not want to impose the 'rape' label on these women. This was not an institutional bias; it was labelling.

The interviews with doctors essentially reported that rape was a 'big word' and they did not want to label it as such. They would only use the word rape if the woman had used it herself. They would not refer or discuss Rape Crisis because that in itself would be labelling what that woman had experienced despite her not having said that. The police were different. If a woman approached the police with the intent for the police to charge the perpetrator then she herself had labelled her experience.

Labelling theory (Lemert, 1981) made even more sense when our group interviewed a spokesperson from Victim Support. They confirmed what DSAC had said. Similar labelling, but to a lesser extent, occurs with the word 'victim.' Labelling theory thus points to the problem with the name Rape Crisis or Victim Support.

In sum, these two studies are different but somewhat identical in the experience that we as first-time researchers had. In the 2015 study, labelling theory pointed to the problem with the name Rape Crisis or Victim Support and in 2014, the class-based survey was problematic. Having discovered this is one thing but there is nothing in the textbooks that tells a novice researcher how to go back to their organisation and tell them something like that. We had both read the papers that the course co-ordinator had written about previous years (Tolich, Paris & Shephard, 2014; Tolich, Shepard, Carson & Hunt, 2013; Tolich, 2013). A feature of each year was how daunting it was to approach the community liaison for the first time, knocking on the door, and acting as if the group were competent researchers. However there was nothing in his reports about having to re-approach the organisation with potentially unsettling news. This was the problem that faced both of us. In what follows we describe what it is like to discover something original and then having to communicate this to the community liaison (Morgan begins, followed by Kayla).

I would describe the 2015 experience finding the label Rape Crisis problematic 'like sherbet dropped in lemonade.' The revelation was mind-blowing. My group came out of the DSAC interview with this new knowledge and had this profound realisation that the entire interview was about the word 'rape' and that we had been looking at the research project through an entirely different and wrong lens. We were excited to have found something that we were not looking for but then we had the responsibility of going back to Rape Crisis with this. Whilst the sherbet had fizzed at first, it then spilled over and got messy. We did not really know how to communicate our findings. The options for putting forward our findings varied: whether to say that there was good news; to call it bad news or to just throw the findings on the table and frame the findings as neutral. We eventually decided on another option; to put forward our findings with a solution—to solve the problem that our findings threw up.

We met with the community liaison in person and we prefaced our opening statement by explaining that we had not found what we had been expecting. She then sat a little further back in her chair. It became clear that a different answer was not only something that had not occurred to us as researchers, but had not occurred to Rape Crisis either. There was a short pause whilst that information sunk in before she asked us what we had found. That experience of watching someone process this unexpected information as we had was another real turning point for us as up until that point we had not considered just how much our findings could affect other people.

We had not been sure how our findings would be received. We were worried especially because coming back with an answer so different felt like coming back with an answer to a different question, one that had not been asked of us. After the initial pause our findings were quickly adopted as a new development. It was a development that attacked a concept that was so firmly attached to Rape Crisis—what the name meant to people—but it was a suggestion that made sense.

Not only did Rape Crisis find the conclusions of our research interesting, but also they concluded that the whole marketing of the organisation might need rethinking. Hearing that they were listening and considering the change showed us that we had the opportunity to change something.

Whereas Morgan describes her research findings as sherbet dropped in lemonade, Kayla's experiences were grounded in trepidation as much as excitement. For Kayla, this was her first original research outcome and like Morgan, she realised that the revelation must be shared with Rape Crisis. Some of my trepidation was rooted in the fact that our comparative analysis of the two schools had been at our own initiative, essentially going beyond the brief. It was only when we had started to examine the results of the surveys that we had contemplated whether to delve deeper and isolate two schools of differing deciles. We consulted with our liaison about this idea and initially they expressed that they did not see whether there was any use breaking down the results further unless we could see any great difference between the schools. Of course we would not be able to see if there was a difference unless we analysed the results so we pressed on and did so, eventually uncovering our unexpected findings. I questioned if we had a right as novice researchers to not only expand our original brief but importantly to voice our findings based on this expansion and to do something that felt as though it was challenging the organisation's way of operating. We too were worried about returning with an answer so different to a question that originally had not been asked of us.

Again like Morgan, it was important that we put forward our findings with a solution, albeit our solution of a revised survey instrument was only a solution in-part. We ended up in a collaboration revising the survey instrument settling on a pre and post survey that measured attitudinal and knowledge change in order to examine the effectiveness of the program. However, it was up to Rape Crisis to decide whether to alter their program depending on the decile rating of the participants. The liaison person was very receptive of our findings and the new surveys and expressed that they appreciated how we had shown interest in the work that Rape Crisis does and helped them in doing so.

As Kayla and Morgan look back on their collective experience, they considered how this Public Sociology course was different to others we had taken during our university careers. Both were faced with a practical predicament and were put into a position where they were accountable to their organisation and also in some ways to the people they serve. They learnt how to view something unexpected as something positive, rather than as a setback, and to see first-hand that research has consequences for other people as well as for us.

In the year since I prompted them to sit down and tape record their stories, Kayla and Morgan have come to the realisation that the research process is not always linear and that unexpected results can lead to difficult but worthwhile conversations with the organisation. Furthermore, the process does not stop once the results have been delineated. The Public Sociology course, unlike other Sociology research papers, does not mimic "real life" but provides an authentic and full research experience. Most of their university experience had been about answering questions based on set answers with little room for discovering something new. Even if a discovery was to be made, no real consequences ensue and the only person potentially changed by the answer is oneself. However, these projects not only changed us but also had the potential to change the lives of others.

Kayla and Morgan's article was submitted for publication and rebuffed as a major revision. Collectively, we addressed these concerns and resubmitted the collective article without my name appearing on it.

Note

1 Permission has been granted by the authors and the journal editor to present the journal in this chapter.

10 Learning outcomes 2012–2017

The lightbulbs turned on in this book are not mine. Many were shared by the students in their reflective journals and interviews with the research assistant. In particular, Chapter 5 records the learning from the community liaisons when I overreached, incorrectly placing my assumptions on them. Ironically, I may have been paid to be the teacher but the students, their community liaisons and the parents provided a great deal of the teaching and the learning outcomes of this course. For that I am grateful.

From the students, I learned depth of insight. A lightbulb moment appeared serendipitously when I wrote letters of recommendation for these students at the end of each year. The recommendations, usually delivered over the phone, were *thick descriptions* of their projects, progress and most importantly the courage they demonstrated in getting through the various stages of the Public Sociology Capstone task.

The students demonstrated tremendous bravery. Collectively, they said that their initial fear which emerged while meeting the liaison person and the participants was real, but that it was ephemeral. The course held other fears to face, too.

Each project was scaffolded around four sequence stages, yet much time was spent in class instructing novice researchers in the myriad of micro etiquette steps of being a professional researcher. We learned experientially by doing research.

In 2014, a lightbulb moment, if not a chandelier moment, helped generate the ethos of the course, separating it from an internship. The change was in the students' perception of their relationship to their organisation. Students had gained a sense of obligation to their organisations after only four weeks; this had previously taken the full 12 weeks of the semester.

This rapid socialisation into taking responsibility for their project was only achieved because of the students' resilience, a willingness to engage with more responsibility after the removal of much of the scaffolding. This extra scaffolding was well intentioned, but it took away essential learning opportunities for these students.

The sense that the students were making a difference for a public good was a reality in their outward orientation to their organisations. This compared with typical conceptions of a traditional inward-looking, self-obsessed internship model.

From the community organisations, I learned that they had few resources to research or to conduct literature reviews and that what they wanted my students to research was singular: Was their organisation relevant? Did it make a difference?

Community liaisons also taught me basic communication skills. They were more likely to be active than passive. Having signed up for the project, they are most likely to want to be involved in all aspects of the research. They needed to be informed of the course schedules, milestones that the students must meet and the marking criteria, as this is what is driving the students' involvement and will help the community manager set aside the time and resources for the students at the appropriate time. To promote this active involvement, community liaisons should be sent materials (the literature review, the information sheet and the interview questions) as they are developed. Students should discuss in advance with the community liaison how the final report will be presented.

From the parents I met in 2008, I learned to question the value of a Sociology degree. Then, I did not have the answers, but now I do. This book attests to that.

From experience and time, I learned much. By the end of 2014, I thought most of the scaffolding had been recognised and dismantled. Yet at the end of 2017, there were other microforms of scaffolding I was yet to realise— not just in the Public Sociology course, but also in the preparatory intermediate research methods course I taught.

There are other lightbulbs yet to discover. A colleague queried my claim that the Public Sociology course is a primer pathway for students towards research careers or social activism. Obviously, the students' self-reports in their reflective journals suggest they have the research skills to follow this employment pathway. But he asked about the experience of the 120 students who had taken the course over the past six years. This could be a research project for me or for future students. Has the Public Sociology course led to pathways to employment or social activism? In the short term, it has been a success to get students to self-report that they acted like researchers, and from my perspective this was endorsed by the community collaborators. I would modify this research question somewhat. Rather than documenting what jobs the students gained, I would rather focus on the actual pathways they took. This framing question encapsulates the philosophy of Public Sociology as outlined in Chapter 2. I was always less interested in destinations and more interested in pathways, especially the micro steps within that pathway.

Appendices

Appendix A: Research proposal for a mixed methods project in year two (this course is the prerequisite for the Public Sociology Capstone)

Your overall task is to develop a funding application that uses a mixed methods framework to persuade an agency (your fellow classmates) to fund your research. The two methods to combine are (1) a survey (questionnaire) and (2) focus groups OR one-on-one interviews. You are not required to either conduct this research or publish the results of this proposal. To prepare the funding application, follow these step-by-step tasks as they incrementally build towards a mixed methods funding application. Complete all seven tasks during the semester. The whole task is worth 100 points or 50% of the final grade. There will be a final exam worth 50%.

Task One: Choose a topic (week two tutorial)

Choose **one** of four topics for your research project. The choices are

1   "self-driving cars";
2   "climate change";
3   "how people get their news";
4   "euthanasia."

This first task requires you to bring your topic selection to the tutorial with a written three-sentence description of why the topic interests you.

Task Two: Construct a 20-item bibliography, due in week four (10 points)

a   Use Harvard citation style
b   Tolich, M. & Davidson, C., 2011. *Getting Started: An Introduction to Research Methods*. Pearson: Auckland.

Task Three: Writing (a tutorial exercise), due in week four (5 points)

Between the bibliography and the literature review it is useful to discover what you think (as the researcher) about your research topic. One good way to do this is "free writing," beginning with "the purpose of the research is …" Write for five minutes without thinking too much about grammar or spelling—you will be surprised what comes up.

Task Four: Literature review, due in week six (20 points)

Compare and contrast ten items from your bibliography and write a single 1000-word statement (not including the bibliography) on how the topic has been researched previously. This literature review also aligns your study to your discipline or to a body of literature, which is important to establish legitimacy for your project. At the end of the statement, write a single sentence under the heading: "My research problem is …"

Task Five: Research design for a questionnaire, due in week eight (20 points)

Use the research question developed in Task Four to construct a series of survey questions.

a   Operationalise the core concept. For example, "where do people get their news?"—which people, what is news.
b   Explain your sampling rationale.
c   Using Survey Monkey, write survey questions that capture both the demographics of the population and a series of substantive questions.
d   Create a series of hypotheses about your research problem linking the dependent variable with each of the four independent variables.

Task Six: Research design for focus groups (20 points)

Use the research question developed in Task Four to construct a series of five focus group questions or a one-on-one interview guide.
   This task has four parts.

1   Explain your sampling rationale.
2   Write a series of five questions that would be used in the focus group or interview.
3   Explain why these questions were created.
4   State the aim of the focus group research.

Task Seven: Seminar presentations, weeks 11 and 12 in tutorial (5 points)

Tasks seven and eight are two parts of the same project. The seminar presentations lasting three minutes are graded on a pass/no pass basis. The questions or comments following the presentation should assist the writing of the final project.

Task Eight: Mixed methods study, due week 13 (20 points)

Write a research proposal using both the survey and focus group questions developed in Tasks 5 and 6 in a single project.

- Give your study a title and subtitle. Perhaps use "A Combined Methods Study" as a subtitle.
- Explain the background of the study by writing a paragraph of about 150 words beginning with *The purpose of the research is ....*
- Include a literature review such as the one developed in Task 4. See this process as iterative, and realise that other articles will be included as the project develops (300 words).
- List the aims and hypotheses of the study developed in Tasks 5 and 6.
- As Task 7 employs both focus groups and survey research techniques, provide the two sets of questions to be asked of informants and respondents. Explain which technique will be used first.
- List two ethical issues that might arise in both the focus groups and the questionnaires and explain how you plan to resolve them (see Chapter 11).
- Provide a justification for the research, sufficient to persuade a funding agency of the merit of your research. Assume the agency will ask, "Well, so what? Why should this study be funded?"
- Part of the justification is achieved by acknowledging that the topic exists within the larger context of the literature. Begin this paragraph by stating *"This project warrants funding because ...."* Do note that the justification has another purpose. The justification is a statement given to the persons invited to take part in your research. Why should they give up their time? Limit the justification to 200 words.

Appendix B: Four-part research proposal for a mixed methods Public Sociology Capstone project

Part One: 10% of final grade (1500 words max)

Write a research protocol inclusive of a literature review, an outline of the research problem, a rationale for choosing the methodology and a justification of why this project is important.

Write the report for an intelligent audience who has no prior knowledge of your project. Make sure to define all of your terms as you proceed. Give your report a tentative working title that captures the meaning of your research question. The literature review should annotate 20 key citations. These will be shared with the community group.

Additionally, write an ethics statement in the form of a Participant Information Sheet. **The course coordinator will take responsibility for gaining ethics approval from the university.** As you can see above, there are a number of tasks that could be divided up and done by individuals or in subgroups.

Part Two: 10% of final grade (1500 words max)

Design the research instrument(s) (i.e. survey, interview guide) and begin coding data.

1   Design the research instrument(s) (i.e. survey, interview guide and/or observation guide.
2   Write a one-page safety plan for the group.
3   Transcribe an observation or an interview you have completed that has been coded. Supply a revised observation or interview guide.
4   Notify the lecturer about the nature of the final output. Is the final output going to be a written report, a video or a poster?

Part Three: 20% of final grade (1500 words max)

Write a preliminary report on how the data were collected and analysed.

1   What is the research question?
2   Provide evidence of your literature review and how it supports the research question(s).
3   Write a brief methodology statement about how you collected and analysed your data.
4   Present evidence that you have begun to write up a number of your thematic themes. **(this is the major task of assignment 3).**

Part Four: 20% of final grade (3000 words max)

The final report revises and resubmits the three previous assignments into a final report that will be given to the community liaison in both written and oral form.

Appendix C: Annotated CV[1]

Bachelor of Arts 2016 in Sociology, University of Otago

My learning and skills development portfolio

Year Three

Theories of Social Power involved understanding a wide variety of Sociological theorists, from Hobbes to Foucault, and applying them to everyday life. Key skills developed were the ability to extract the core meaning from these works and present them in a concise writing style.

Mixed Methods gave me an understanding and application of both quantitative and qualitative methods of Sociological research, inclusive of statistical analysis by way of Chi-squared tests.

Governing Bodies centred around how theorists, such as Hobbes and Nietzsche, view the state and the way it enforces population control. The key skill developed was the ability to summarise and interpret large bodies of work through a parliamentary debate report as well a group presentation on feminist critiques of the state.

Masculinities analysed the work of various academics of masculinity such as Polk and Ranson as well as the historical evolution of both masculinity and the theory of masculinity. Key skills gained were the ability to generate topics of discussion as well as formulating an argument based on literature.

Gender, Work and Consumer Culture. The learning involved in this course was based largely on the theory and study of consumer culture as well as the effect that gender and work have on a consumer culture, and vice versa. Key skills that I gained from this course were the ability to plan, conduct, analyse and then write a report based on an interview on my chosen topic.

Year Two

Research Methods. The learning was a theoretical introduction to the methods of conducting Sociological research as well as the construction of a research proposal. Skills developed were conducting a literature review, creating mixed methods survey and focus group questions and defence of the research proposal.

Critical Victimology engaged with critical analyses of victimology, both feminist or positivist, and the contributing factors that lead to victimisation. My writing style was enhanced through analysing victim narratives, problem solving and generating original research questions.

Crime, Justice and Society offered an introduction to the study of crime such as the societal view of crime as a whole as well as the factors in life that lead to crime. A course emphasised teamwork in creating and performing an oral presentation in a group environment.

Islam, Politics and the Challenge of Terrorism offered an insight into the basics of the Islamic culture as well as the misrepresentation of Islam as a form of terrorism, from which Islamophobia stems. Key skills gained were case study analysis within a tutorial setting as well as the creation and formulation of an essay topic and argument.

Concepts of the Self highlighted our ability or struggle for agency in a modern setting, drawing on theoretical approaches ranging from Giddens to Goffman. Key skills gained were the ability to summarise and relay bodies of text both orally and in writing.

Social Inequality. The learning was based around the positive and negative effects of social inequality within the NZ setting. This course also has a focus on the theoretical approaches to social inequality, such as intersectionality and conflict theories. The key skill gained in this course was the ability to apply theories of social inequality to an essay of a chosen case study within the NZ context.

Year One

Introductory Sociology Papers offered a broad look at the study of Sociology in terms of theorists, theories and literature. These foundation courses introduced the expected style of writing that would be used throughout all following Sociology courses. The key skills were basic: how to summarise and apply literature to a chosen topic in order to formulate an argument.

Statistical Methods gave an understanding of different forms of data distribution, such as binomial, as well as analysing and drawing conclusions from data sets. This basic understanding of analysing statistics was later applied in third-year courses.

Introductory Psychology Papers focused on a broad introduction to the discipline. A key skill gained was the comprehension of a different approach to developing a written report than Sociology.

Appendix D: Possible structure of a verbal presentation

In 2017, each team of students was required to make a joint presentation of their project to invited community liaisons and faculty. In preparation for these talks, I asked each group to preload their PowerPoint slides before practicing their presentation in the penultimate class. It quickly became apparent that the students had done no practice working as a team to ensure that they finished their talk under the allocated five-minute time limit. Moreover, they showed little experience in presenting a project in a public forum. After two presentations had failed to get beyond the literature review within five minutes, I halted proceedings and improvised the format below that encouraged them to "speak to" their projects rather than either reading the slides out or attempting to describe everything from the research question to the research output. It appeared as if the students collectively couldn't distinguish the wheat from the chaff, as everything seemed important. I scribbled the following nine-point sequence on the classroom's whiteboard:

1   Your first PowerPoint slide should provide a title, maybe also a subtitle. Together they capture the essence of the project in retrospect. There is no need to read it out. Include your full names on slide one.

2   Begin the talk by introducing the organisation rather than the liaison person and tell the audience what the problem was that the organisation wanted studied. Maybe even the format of the final written or video outcome.

3   Next, have a slide titled "literature review" and list 2–3 key sources. This usually ends with announcing the research question or research problem that is theoretically informed.

4   Very briefly discuss any ethical issues, but only if there anything unusual. Mention that you wrote a safety plan and describe a feature of it in one sentence. The main point is that the project was ethical and you were safe.

5   Discuss the recruitment or sampling of your participants—how you contacted them and how many you interviewed or surveyed. Note, if using mixed methods, that the survey and the interviews should be

made distinct. [*The first five parts of the talk should take no more than 2 of the 5 minutes. There is no room to adlib—that can be done in question time.*]

6   The next stage is the most important for any presentation. Try using an organising sentence such as "*Analysis of the 10 interviews highlighted three core themes.*" On a slide, show them as X, Y and Z. On the next three slides present the data around these X, Y and Z themes separately.

7   In your own words describe X and then provide one or two short quotes from an informant that highlights X. If possible, make a transition to Y. For example, while all informants said X, a number said Y.

8   Findings or Discussion: wrap up the talk by linking the original research problem or research question thrown up by the literature review with the findings from the three themes above.

9   Finally, offer recommendations that go in two directions. What one thing do you want to tell the organisation? The other direction is what future students could research in this area. End by thanking the community liaison and ask if anyone in the audience has questions.

Appendix E: Typical safety plan

Because our research project is qualitative, we will be conducting interviews with participants. It is therefore crucial to have safety measures in place to ensure that we are comfortable and do not place ourselves in danger. The first and primary feature of our safety plan is that somebody will always know where and at what times we will be conducting the interviews.

Additionally, our transportation and the places in which we interview the participants are important features of our safety plan. With two members of the team owning a car as well as full drivers' licences, we are ensured to have a secure mode of transport to travel to the interview location and a way of leaving if we do not feel safe. Our interviews are also conducted in public places with multiple people close by, outside of the interview room. For instance, one of our interviews was conducted at a church. Several employees and volunteers were in the building during the interview. This was a safe location as we were ensured that, if something untoward were to happen, other people would be there to assist.

Another feature of our safety plan is ensuring that we have more than one member of the group present during the interview. As we are a group of three, we have decided that to conduct the research efficiently, we should interview in pairs. Having two people present at the interview increases our sense of security and our safety. Ideally, by having more than one person, we will less likely be victims of any sort of harm during the interview.

Professionalism through both our behaviour and appearance is also an important safety measure. Maintaining professionalism ensures that we are not acting or dressing in any suggestive or provocative way that may potentially jeopardise the interview process. To dress professionally, we all wear pants and a loose fitting, high-cut top that is neat and clean. This conservative attire gives the impression that we will take the interview and the participant seriously while ensuring that we do not look naive.

Finally, our cell phones are an essential safety item we will always have during the interview. These phones are usually placed on the table in front of us and are recording everything that is said during the interview. The phones are also useful as a scapegoat if either of the interviewers are feeling uncomfortable at any stage. Prior to the interviews, both interviewers will discuss the potential to pretend to receive an emergency phone call if they feel the need to leave.

Appendix F: Example of a student's ethnographic accounted posted on the organisation website

Observing Miss Daisy (2016)[2]

Three students from the University of Otago were given the opportunity to ride along separately with North Dunedin Driving Miss Daisy (DMD) as they ferried customers to and from meetings, appointments, shopping and outings. The focus of the observation was the driver of the elder care transportation service. Invariably the passengers, all anonymous, at times came into focus.

The field notes taken by the students from the back seat of the car revealed three themes: independence, isolation and emotional labour. The following is evidence of the students' third draft that was edited by me for final presentation to their manager. Their observations found that Driving Miss Daisy shares few similarities with a normal taxi service. What makes this service invaluable to the mostly female passengers aged between 65 and 90 years old was how it created independent living for those customers living with chronic health problems, the loss of friends and the loss of mobility.

Many of the customers experienced some form of social isolation. One customer was extremely appreciative that the driver took them via the main street through town so they could observe the city and appreciate simple things, such as the changing autumn leaves. It appeared to casual observers that the customers did not get out often.

The driver knew the passengers very well and was part of their lives. The driver asked a passenger if they would be receiving a regular phone call over the weekend. This recognition excited the person, and the conversation for the majority of the journey focused on the joy that the passenger got from this phone call.

The driver played multiple roles. Although this emotional labour must have been tiring, the driver appeared to have a satisfaction knowing she was making a difference to a client's day. For example, on one observation the driver played the role of a grief counsellor. At the beginning of this journey the driver enquired about the well-being of the client upon hearing a loved one had passed away, the driver consoled the client as they reminisced. The driver's ability to give uplifting and encouraging comments was not only observed in this instance, but also in the other observations.

While, the driver would listen to intimate details of the client, the clients would also make enquiries on the well-being of the driver or the well-being of members of the DMD 'family.' From the observations it was evident that two-way emotional labour was occurring—where both the driver and the client would listen to and empathise with one another. For example, the majority of clients asked how the driver was, with several clients also concerned about the health of one of the DMD employees who had undergone surgery. Clients have the option to request a particular driver, this was obviously based on the relationship that they had with the driver. Due to this intimate relationship between the driver and client no two days were the same. Terms used such as 'my client' or 'regular client' represented the personalised relationship that the driver had with each of the clients.

Whilst the majority of the observed clients had mobility issues, there were a variety of reasons why clients chose to use this service. These included: cessation of driver's license, recent surgeries, parking concerns and aging concerns. One client was grateful to Driving Miss Daisy as she had been diagnosed with macular degeneration in the last 4 or 5 years meaning she could no longer drive.

Drivers treat each client as an individual and find ways to enhance their independence. They gauged the level of support needed to assist the clients on their journey with DMD. This ensured there was never any unnecessary help given—allowing the clients to keep their independence. For example, a client had his courtship independence enhanced. DMD picked him up and then drove to his wife's rest home allowing the client to take his wife on a date. On these journeys the driver played nothing more than the assigned driver role.

One driver, a former taxi driver, enjoyed this personalised type service. A feature of the service was the adequate time allowed. Evident through the opening of car doors, courteously fastening seat belts and the door-to-door service offered. Unlike a taxi service, there was no meter used that could potentially pressure the client, instead a private logbook was kept recording the distance driven. The greatest difference between this service and a taxi service was the relationships between the driver and the client.

The Driving Miss Daisy North Dunedin franchise continually strives to uphold its customer service towards their client base. The efforts made by the driver in fulfilling the needs of their clientele reiterates their quote 'we're there for you.' From the observations, DMD provided clients an opportunity to be part of society and addressed the common issue of isolation amongst elderly. The service also helped maintain the independence of clients and established physical and emotional support between drivers and clients. DMD is an invaluable service that provides affordable transportation and most importantly companionship thus becomes a surrogate family for the clients.

Notes

1 Permission has been granted by the student who wrote this CV to present it here.
2 The owner of the Driving Miss Daisy company has given permission for this excerpt to be presented here.

References

"A Code of Practice for the Safety of Social Researchers." (n.d.). Social Research Association. www.the-sra.org.uk/wp-content/uploads/safety_code_of_practice. pdf. Accessed June 9, 2011.

Allen, K., Quinn, J., Hollingworth, S. & Rose, A. (2013). Becoming employable students and 'ideal' creative workers: Exclusion and inequality in higher education work placements. *British Journal of Sociology of Education*, 34(3): 431–452.

Apple, M.W. (2006). *Educating the "Right" Way: Markets, Standards. God, and Inequality*. New York: Taylor & Francis.

Bach, R. & Weinzimmer, J. (2011). Exploring the benefits of community-based research in a sociology of sexualities course. *Teaching Sociology*, 39(1): 57–72.

"BA Capstone Planning." (n.d.). Department of Sociology, Humboldt University. Accessed October 24, 2017. http://www2.humboldt.edu/sociology/BA_Capstone.

Ball, L., Pollard, E. & Stanley, N. (2010). *Creative Graduates Creative Futures*. CGCF Higher Education. http://www.employment-studies.co.uk/sites/default/files/471sum.pdf.

Becker, H.S. (1974). Labelling theory reconsidered. In Rock, P. & Mcintosh, M. (eds.). *Deviance and Social Control*. London: Tavistock, pp. 41–66.

Bellah, R., Madsen, R., Sullivan, W.M., Swidler, A. & Tipton, S.M. (1985). *Habits of the Heart*. Berkeley, CA: University of California Press.

Bendix, R. (1962). *Max Weber: An Intellectual Portrait*. New York: Anchor.

Berger, P.L. (1963). *Invitation to Sociology. A Humanistic Sociology*. Garden City, NY: Doubleday.

Bernstein, B. (1975). *Class, Codes and Control: Towards a Theory of Educational Transmissions*. London: Routledge and Kegan Paul.

Bourdieu, P. (2010). *Sociology is a Martial Art: Political Writings by Pierre Bourdieu*. G. Sapiro (ed.). New York: New Press.

Briggs, F. & Hawkins, M.R. (1994). Follow-up data on the effectiveness of New Zealand's national school-based child protection program. *Child Abuse and Neglect*, 18(8): 635–643.

Bronner, S.E. & Kellner, D.M. (1989). *Critical Theory and Society: A Reader*. New York: Routledge.

Burawoy, M. (2004). American Sociological Association presidential address: For public sociology. *British Journal of Sociology*, 56(2): 259–294.

Burawoy, M., Gamson, W., Ryan, C., Pfohl, S., Vaughan, D., Derber, C. & Schor, J. (2004). Public sociologies: A symposium from Boston College. *Social Problems*, 51(1): 103–130. https://doi.org/10.1525/sp.2004.51.1.103.

Burawoy, M. (2005). For public sociology. *American Sociological Review*, 70(1): 4–28. Centre for Human Services Technology. "Defining research mindedness." http://www.resmind.swap.ac.uk/.

"Career Paths with Sociology." (n.d.). Accessed October 24, 2017. https://sociology.ucsd.edu/undergraduate/career-paths.html.

Cook, K. (2011). Presidential address: Realizing the promise of sociology: Going public and enriching community. *Sociation Today*, 9(1): 7. www.ncsociology.org/sociationtoday/v91/profess.htm.

Davis, N. (1993). Bringing it all together: The sociological imagination. *Teaching Sociology*, 21(3): 233–238.

Du Bois, W.E.B. (1903). *The Souls of Black Folk*. New York: A.C. McClurg.

Dunedin Public Libraries – Bookbus Service." (n.d.). Accessed October 24, 2017. https://www.youtube.com/watch?v=9RYoZtpybSk.

Editorial. (2007). 5 May. The Christchurch Press, A21.

Fine, G.A. (1979). Small groups and culture creation: The idioculture of little league baseball teams. American Sociological Review, 44(5): 733–745.

Fine, G.A. (1987). *With the Boys: Little League Baseball and Preadolescent Culture*. Chicago: University of Chicago Press.

Finkelstein, M. (2009). Toward teaching a liberating sociological practicality: Challenges for teaching, learning and practice. *Teaching Sociology*, 37(1): 89–102.

"Graduate Incomes to Be Published." (2012). Accessed October 24, 2017. http://www.stuff.co.nz/dominion-post/news/politics/6566601/Graduate-incomes-to-be-published.

Geuss, R. (1981). *The Idea of a Critical Theory: Habermas and the Frankfurt School*. New York: Cambridge University Press.

Goffman, E. (1961). *Asylums*. London: Pelican Books.

Habermas, J. (1972). *Knowledge and Human Interests*. London: Heinemann.

Harford, T. (2016). *Messy: How to be Creative and Resilient in a Tidy-Minded World*. London: Little, Brown Book Group.

Hauhart, R.C. & Grahe, J.E. (2015). *Designing and Teaching Undergraduate Capstone Courses*. San Francisco: Jossey-Bass.

Hochschild, A. (1983). *The Managed Heart*. Berkeley: University of California Press.

Holton, W. (2005). "Sociology Senior Seminar – Course Outline and Requirements." Northeastern University. https://www.northeastern.edu/cssh/socant/wp-content/uploads/sites/19/2014/09/SOC-600-Spring-2005-syllabus.pdf.

"Income Premiums for Study Options Revealed." (n.d.). *The Beehive*. Accessed October 24, 2017. http://www.beehive.govt.nz/release/income-premiums-study-options-revealed.

Johnston, J. (2011). Interrogating the goals of work-integrated learning: Neoliberal agendas and critical pedagogy. *Asia-Pacific Journal of Cooperative Education*, 12(3): 175–182.

Kelsey, J. (1995). *The New Zealand Experiment: A World Model for Structural Adjustment*. Auckland: Auckland University Press.

Krueger, R. (n.d.). "Moderating Focus Groups." Accessed October 24, 2017. https://www.youtube.com/watch?v=xjHZsEcSqwo.

Kuh, G.D., Schneider, C.G. & Association of American Colleges and Universities. (2008). *High-Impact Educational Practices: What They Are, Who Has Access To Them, and Why They Matter*. Washington, DC: Association of American Colleges and Universities.

Lawton, K. & Potter, D. (2010). *Why Interns Need a Fair Wage*. London: Institute for Public Policy Research.

"Lao Tzu Quotes." (n.d.). BrainyQuote. Accessed October 24, 2017. https://www.brainyquote.com/quotes/quotes/l/laotzu137141.html.

Lemert, E.M. (1981). Issues in the study of deviance. *The Sociological Quarterly*, 22(2): 285–305.

"Master of Arts in Public Sociology Courses." (n.d.). University of the Rockies. Accessed October 24, 2017. https://www.rockies.edu/degrees/ma-public-sociology-courses.htm.

McKenzie, D. (1999). The clouded trail: Ten years of public education post-Picot. *New Zealand Journal of Educational Studies*, 34(1): 8–17.

Mills, C.W. (2000). *The Sociological Imagination*. New York: Oxford University Press.

Morello, G. (n.d.). "Sociology Senior Seminar." Boston College. https://www.bc.edu/content/dam/files/schools/cas_sites/sociology/pdf/2014S/SC455Morello.pdf.

Norris, J., Sawyer, R.D. & Lund, D. (2012). *Duoethnography: Dialogic Methods for Social, Health, and Educational Research* (Vol. 7). Walnut Creek, CA: Left Coast Press.

Perlin, R. (2012). *Intern Nation: How to Earn Nothing and Learn Little in the Brave New Economy*. London: Verso Books.

Riesman, D. (1950). *The Lonely Crowd: A Study of the Changing American Character*. New Haven, CT: Yale University Press.

Ross, A. (2009). *Nice Work If You Can Get It: Life and Labor in Precarious Times*. New York: New York University Press.

Scott, J.C. (2008). *Weapons of the Weak: Everyday Forms of Peasant Resistance*. New Haven, CT: Yale University Press.

Seybold, P. (n.d.). "Capstone FAQ." Sociology Department IUPUI. http://liberalarts.iupui.edu/sociology/uploads/docs/CapstoneFAQs.pdf.

Sieber, J.E. and Tolich, M.B. (2013). *Planning Ethically Responsible Research* (Vol. 31). Thousand Oaks, CA: Sage.

"Sociology Is a Martial Art." (n.d.) Accessed October 24, 2017. http://www.icarusfilms.com/if-socio.

"Sociology – The University of Auckland." (n.d.). Accessed October 24, 2017. http://www.arts.auckland.ac.nz/en/about/subjects-and-courses/sociology.html.

"Sociology Department at Clark University." (n.d.). Accessed October 24, 2017. https://www2.clarku.edu/departments/sociology/.

Spalter-Roth, R., Senter, M.S., Stone, P. & Wood, M. (2010). ASA's Bachelor's and Beyond Survey: Findings and their implications for students and departments. *Teaching Sociology*, 38(4): 314–329.

Stewart, K. & Speight, M. (2016). Examining rape crisis practice: A Public Sociology duoethnography. *New Zealand Sociology*, 31(1): 181–189.

Swan, E. (2015). The internship class: Subjectivity and inequalities – gender, race and class. In Broadbridge A.M. & Fielden S.L. (eds.). *Handbook of Gendered Careers in Management: Getting In, Getting On, Getting Out*. Cheltenham, UK: Edward Elgar, pp. 30–43.

"Teacher Education Timetables, Orientation and Course Groups." (n.d.) University of Canterbury. Accessed October 24, 2017. http://www.canterbury.ac.nz/education/student-advice-and-forms/timetables/.

"The GROW Model: A Simple Process for Coaching and Mentoring." (n.d.). Accessed October 24, 2017. http://www.mindtools.com/pages/article/newLDR_89.htm.

Thomas, W.I. (1923). *The Unadjusted Girl*. London: Harper and Row.

Tolich, M. (2012a). Sociology graduates require pathways, not employment destinations: The promise of experiential learning. *New Zealand Journal of Sociology*, 27(2): 148–158.

Tolich, M. (2012b). My eye-opening midnight swim: An Outward Bound autoethnography. *New Zealand Journal of Outdoor Education: Ko Tane Mahuta Pupuke*, 3(1): 9–23.

Tolich, M. (2015). Facilitating research mindedness in a sociology research internship course. In van Heugten, K. & Gibbs, A. (eds.). *Social Work for Sociologists: Theory and Practice*. New York: Palgrave Macmillan, pp. 157–170.

Tolich M. & Davidson, C. (2011). *Getting Started: An Introduction to Research Methods*. Auckland: Pearson Education.

Tolich, M., Paris, A. & Shephard, K. (2014). An evaluation of experiential learning in a sociology internship class. *New Zealand Sociology*, 29(1): 119–134.

Tolich, M., Scarth, B. & Shephard, K. (2015). Teaching sociology students to become qualitative-researchers using an internship model of learner-support. *Journal of Social Science Education*, 14(4): 53–63.

Tolich, M., Shephard, K., Carson, S. & Hunt, D. (2013). Co-managing the sustainability of University internship programs in brownfield sites. *New Zealand Sociology*, 28(1): 156–170.

Tryon, E. & Stoecker, R. (2008). The unheard voices: Community organizations and service-learning. *Journal of Higher Education Outreach and Engagement*, 12(3): 47–60.

"UIC SOC 490 Capstone." (n.d.). University of Illinois at Chicago. Accessed October 24, 2017. https://soc.uic.edu/sociology/undergraduate/soc-490-capstone-project.

Yee, K. (2008). *Mouse Trap: Memoir of a Disneyland Cast Member*. Orlando: Ultimate Orlando Press.

Index

University of Canterbury *see* Canterbury University programs
University of Illinois in Chicago 13
University of Otago: Sociology department 3, 5, 11–12; *see also* Science Wananga Project
University of the Rockies 13

verbal reports 29

Weber, M. 11
Weinzimmer, J. 11
work integrated learning program 1–2
Wriggle and Rhyme project 51–54

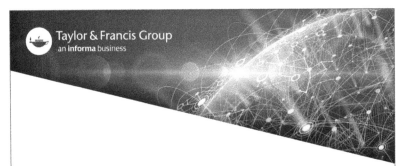

For Product Safety Concerns and Information please contact our EU
representative GPSR@taylorandfrancis.com
Taylor & Francis Verlag GmbH, Kaufingerstraße 24, 80331 München, Germany

www.ingramcontent.com/pod-product-compliance
Ingram Content Group UK Ltd.
Pitfield, Milton Keynes, MK11 3LW, UK
UKHW021422080625
459435UK00011B/114